VISUAL

99 PROVEN WAYS FOR SMALL BUSINESSES TO MARKET WITH IMAGES AND DESIGN

DAVID LANGTON AND ANITA CAMPBELL

MARKETING

VISUAL

99 PROVEN WAYS FOR SMALL BUSINESSES TO MARKET WITH IMAGES AND DESIGN

DAVID LANGTON AND ANITA CAMPBELL

MARKETING

WILEY

John Wiley & Sons, Inc.

Published by John Wiley & Sons, Inc., Hoboken, New Jersey.
Published simultaneously in Canada.

For general information on our other products and services or for technical support, please contact our Customer Care Department within the United States at (800) 762-2974, outside the United States at (317) 572-3993 or fax (317) 572-4002.

Wiley also publishes its books in a variety of electronic formats. Some content that appears in print may not be available in electronic books. For more information about Wiley products, visit our web site at www.wiley.com.

Library of Congress Cataloging-in-Publication Data:

Langton, David, 1961–

Visual marketing : 99 proven ways for small businesses to market with images and design / David Langton, Anita Campbell. — 1
    p. cm.
ISBN 978-1-118-03567-2 (paper); ISBN 978-1-118-14369-8 (ebk); ISBN 978-1-118-14367-4 (ebk); ISBN 978-1-118-14368-1 (ebk)
1. Small business marketing. 2. Marketing—Graphic methods. I. Campbell, Anita, 1956– II. Title.
HF5415.13.L343   2011
658.8—dc23

2011021455

Printed in the United States of America

10 9 8 7 6 5 4 3 2 1

CONTENTS

Chapter 1

Much More than Just a Website
How Online Games, Cartoons, Apps, Infographics, and More Can Boost Your Business

Chapter 2

Images Are Everywhere in the Physical World
Signs, Banners, Giveaways, Packaging, and Experiential Marketing
That Inspire and Persuade

Chapter 3

Power to the Print Item!
Posters, Brochures, Postcards, and Logos
Still Pack a Punch in the Internet Age

ACKNOWLEDGMENTS

To Norman Cherubino, principal and cofounder of Langton Cherubino Group, Ltd., for his visual acumen and ability to discern what projects exemplify the best in visual marketing. Norman serves as the chief researcher for the book, and without his contributions, this book would never have been completed.

To Susan Payton, president of Egg Marketing & Communications, for her tireless efficiency in pulling together the information for the 99 examples and for her creativity in technical editing. Susan serves as our technical editor, and without her, this book surely would have taken far longer.

Thanks To

Kathi Elster, for sharing her experience and insight as a marketer and author; Jim Keller, for his wit, eloquence, and supreme visual intelligence; Veronica Sozek, my first art teacher, for inspiring me to think visually; Richard Walsh, who was the first small-business owner to influence me; and Peg Patterson, Hannah Shatz, and Teri Scheinzeit, for serving as my gurus when Norman and I started Langton Cherubino Group.

I descended from a small-business owner and a typesetter who set type by hand. My maternal grandfather, Walter Walsh, founded his own flower shop in Woonsocket, Rhode Island; lost it in the Depression; and rebuilt it again. My paternal grandfather set type for the *Providence Journal* and edited the *Fox Point Rambler* during WWII. Both influenced my destiny.

Thanks to our editor Dan Ambrosio and editorial assistant, Ashley Allison at John Wiley & Sons, Inc. Kudos to Geoff Williams, who wrote about me in Entreprenuer.com, and thanks to Peter Shankman for creating HARO.

I would like to thank my parents, Austin and Carol, for their never-ending encouragement and support. I dedicate this book to the ones who have seen me at my best and worst and everything in between: Rachael, Jae Min, and my one and only, Shelley.

—David Langton, May 2011

How do you start giving thanks in a book with so many ideas like this? It's like trying to bottle up the atmosphere—an impossibly large task. Each day in my travels on the Web and to events across the United States, with countless interactions with talented people, I am inspired. I couldn't possibly name everyone I've learned from (I'd need half a book just for acknowledgments!), but there are a few people I would like to single out.

John Jantsch of Duct Tape Marketing has taught me a lot about marketing and given me pointers on book authoring. Ivana Taylor of DIYMarketers.com taught me how to break down marketing ideas into achievable projects on a small-business budget: after talking with her *anything* seems doable. Aaron Wall of SEOBook.com runs an online community where I met some of the entrepreneurs profiled in the book and where I've learned much about the art of presenting information on the Web. And then there's my dedicated staff: Staci Wood, Amanda Stillwagon, and Marie Hernan, along with the outside professionals we work with. You know who you are. And, of course, there are the many thousands of small-business owners and entrepreneurs I've run into on Twitter, Facebook, and in my travels—especially the loyal readers of SmallBizTrends.com and BizSugar.com. It's because of you that I can't wait to get to my computer in the morning.

Special thanks go to Dan Ambrosio, our editor, who kept after me to write a book. The odd irony is that I write so much each day online that I never thought I'd find the time to write a book. Then one day Dan introduced me to my coauthor, David Langton, in a Starbucks (where else?) near Grand Central Terminal in New York. From that fateful meeting, this book took shape. Much appreciation to our editorial assistant Ashley Allison and the rest of the people at Wiley for supporting us, too.

A quick nod to Wufoo, 37 Signals, and Google Apps: without your virtual collaboration tools our book team (spread out literally from sea to shining sea) could not have functioned.

Last, but most important to me, is my husband, Kevin, who has put up with my long hours but is always there. You're my rock. I draw strength from you more than you know.

—Anita Campbell, May 2011

INTRODUCTION

This book is an idea starter. Expect this book to stimulate your senses. Inspire you. Spark ideas. The 99 hand-picked examples in *Visual Marketing* are from organizations just like yours that have successfully used visual elements in their marketing—with solid results.

Why "Visual" Marketing?

The world is visual. We use our eyes to take in much of the content that influences our behavior, tempers our reactions, and informs our decisions. Whether it's on the Web, in a brochure, or live in person, the most effective solutions are ones that unexpectedly grab our attention.

Thousands of books about marketing have been written, including many good ones. Few, however, focus specifically on that intersection point between design (the visual) and marketing (influencing buying behavior), or do so on a scale that small businesses will find relevant. Yet there's never been a better time in history for small businesses to explore using electronic, print, and three-dimensional visuals. Technology puts it within the reach of small businesses to use visuals in our marketing—visuals that previously only the largest corporations could cost-effectively design and implement. The Internet makes it convenient to find and hire design professionals to collaborate with to achieve your marketing goals. And for the do-it-yourselfers, today's online software services and design tools make it easy to experiment with creating visual elements on your own.

What's Inside

Visual Marketing is a compendium of marketing tips and ideas. We looked at more than 500 examples and selected them for practicality, creativity, inspiration, and variety. For us, the key was finding projects that not only looked good but had a good return on investment for the business.

We sought out projects from all across the United States and internationally. You will find sophisticated projects that reveal the hand of talented designers, using visual intelligence in unexpected ways. You will also find simple smart projects requiring minimal resources that solo entrepreneurs executed. The examples range from technology-oriented solutions such as the QR code–enabled three-dimensional displays and posters for the Warhol Factory Party in Alaska to a can of "nothing" produced in Rhode Island to combat hunger. Some solutions are clever and complex, such as the cardboard record player that GGRP created to build buzz for its recording business. Others are as uncomplicated as a head shot taken with a handful of colorful Sharpie markers, like that of Michelle Villalobos when she redefined her personal brand.

We've divided the book into three chapters. The first focuses on Web and electronic solutions. The second features packaging, exhibits, and tangible three-dimensional marketing devices in the physical world. The third encompasses print solutions and logos/branding pieces. Each example ends in a Takeaway Tip distilling the examples into ideas and lessons for small-business people to put to work.

Visual Marketing is a compendium of winning ideas intended to inspire small-business leaders, creative professionals, entrepreneurs, and students. We hope it inspires you to think up your own ideas for incorporating visuals into your marketing.

Chapter 1

MUCH MORE THAN JUST A WEBSITE: HOW ONLINE GAMES, CARTOONS, APPS, INFOGRAPHICS, AND MORE CAN BOOST YOUR BUSINESS

The World Wide Web and e-mail were just the beginning of online marketing. In this chapter we show you how successful visual marketing accomplishes a variety of objectives and takes multiple forms today.

Join us as we explore how social networking sites such as Facebook and the world of mobile apps have redefined how people communicate. Explore a fabrics showroom without leaving your home or office through the intuitive navigation techniques of a great website such as CarnegieFabrics.com.

Some projects are all about technology yet take a relatively low-tech approach. Expert Laser Services knows all about the latest in printing technology, but instead of pushing technology, they used a YouTube contest about destroying printers to build their marketing. And some like GoldRun use the latest technology to insert an image into a virtual reality—whereas Two Leaves and a Bud Tea Company uses stunning photography of tea farmers to distinguish its brand from its much larger competitors.

And just when you think you have all forms of marketing figured out, new marketing technology such as QR codes come along as technology evolves. We show you more than 30 examples of online visual marketing—ranging from simple to sophisticated—all to help you boost business without an exorbitant information technology (IT) budget.

1. The Color of Money: A Small Bank Makes a Large Impression with a Colorful Campaign

Can a small local bank take on the giant conglomerates and win? Norway Savings Bank in Maine saw an opportunity in the economic downturn. They set out to woo small business clients in a state where a majority of employment is tied to small business.

Why It Works

The Colorful Solutions campaign with photography by David McLain of Aurora Novus showcases Norway Savings, a local bank, that proudly announces: "We're from Maine—our roots go back to the 1800s." They combine the familiar, friendly, and homespun wisdom of Maine with the expertise and financial acumen of full-service institutions. The campaign, created by Leslie Evans Design Associates, features profiles of six Maine business owners delivered in print advertisements, on the website, and in radio commercials, as well as in six 30-second videos shown on local television and via YouTube. Evans says the success is really about credibility. "We didn't want to color things—but actually shoot real people with real items in color."

Green is for Mike Skillin, the chief financial officer of Skillin's Greenhouse. Brown is for Andy Charles, proprietor of Haven's Candy, a Maine landmark. The stories show how each business owner benefits from the personal attention and wide resources of Norway Savings. Karen Hakala, the bank's senior vice president of marketing, says that Norway Savings wanted to be the bank of choice for small business, so they created a point of differentiation with their Colorful Solutions campaign.

Success Metrics

- Since the Colorful Solutions campaign was introduced, the business side of the bank has experienced double-digit deposit growth.
- The campaign won the Best of Show award from the American Bankers' Association.
- The Colorful Solutions campaign really resonates with people. Norway Savings has a customer retention rate exceeding 92 percent.

Takeaway Tip

Using customer testimonials and featuring customer stories are time-honored ways to bring to life the value of the products and services you deliver. But why not kick it up a level and use visual clues to further emphasize the range of customer needs you can serve?

2. A Website Showcases a Sense of Touch: Strong Navigation and Ease of Use for an Online Showroom

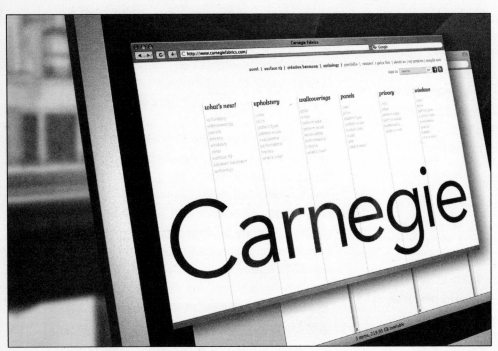

How do you get to Carnegie Fabrics? The usual practice of visiting the showroom is no longer the only way to see and choose fabrics. The website has become the new destination and growing sales tool for this family-owned business. The need for an effective website is essential for the future of an industry where face time is dwindling and decisions need to be made without a trip to the showroom. Carnegie needed to show an extensive collection of merchandise while maintaining its highly regarded service and ease of browsing that clients are accustomed to in their physical showrooms.

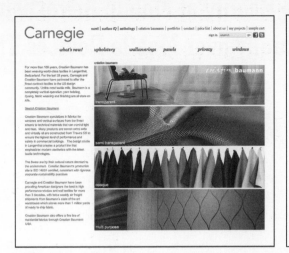

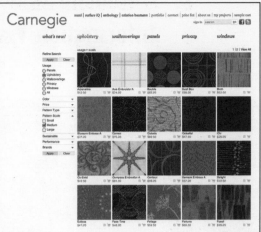

Why It Works

The website features a white screen with a larger rendering of the Carnegie logo. As you roll over the contents that are listed in neat columns, the patterns of different fabrics are revealed within the letters of the Carnegie logo. The primary audience consists of interior designers and architects who are looking for the highest-quality products for their clients. The Carnegie website allows the user to view the wide array of products and color/fabric swatches in a quick and straightforward manner. The details in the photography show off the textures of the materials. The previous versions of the website were more along the lines of an online brochure; with this incarnation users have the ability to order samples, search products, access product information, and see the details of the fabrics.

Success Metrics

- Traffic to the new Carnegie Fabrics website has increased 10 percent.
- The number of samples requested online has increased 15 percent.
- By increasing the amount of online sample order transactions, Carnegie has printed significantly fewer marketing materials and further enhanced its status as an eco-friendly company.

Takeaway Tip

Your customers online expect the same level of service that they experience "offline."

Examine the navigation and ease of use of your website to be sure the level of detail and functionality are there for online users. Instead of laying out your site like a static brochure, mimic the experience of being in your office as much as possible, including the experience of browsing merchandise and getting personalized help. When you are in an industry of tactile goods, it's especially important to have as close a substitute for the real thing as you can, with detailed photographs and descriptions.

3. Augmenting the Reality of Mobile Advertising: Sharing Brand Information Visually over Mobile Devices Through Apps

In a world where sites like Foursquare, Facebook Places, and Gowalla are vying for the attention of retailers and corporations, lesser-known GoldRun is actually getting it. The company is augmenting reality to get users to engage with a brand.

Users of the GoldRun app see virtual objects superimposed over real-world places where they look with their iPhone cameras. For example, in a promotion for *Esquire* magazine, a super model "appears" near the newsstand aisle at a Barnes and Noble bookstore. The idea is that it will "drive traffic to physical and online destinations, increase product sales, enhance brand engagement and bolster viral impact," says Lucy Swope of GoldRun.

Why It Works

Advertisers are still struggling with the idea of going mobile in their advertising. With GoldRun, users are excited to participate and uncover secrets only they know about. It turns advertising into an experience where the advertising brand is engaged.

Because it appeals to "a wide spectrum of people from film buffs and fashion devotees, to sports fans, deal seekers and vacationers," according to Swope, GoldRun's app will never get old, as runs are finite and new challenges are being added constantly.

Success Metrics

- GoldRun has seen on average 500 to 1,000 downloads/followed runs per week for runs that are being actively promoted.

- Client Airwalk sold out of the limited edition sneakers featured in their invisible pop-up stores and had the busiest weekend ever on their website following its GoldRun promotion.
- The company continues to add on high-profile clients such as Sorel, H&M, and Esquire.

Takeaway Tip

Mobile advertising and the mobile Web are changing how people interact with the world around them. You can now communicate about your brand over consumers' small handheld devices while they are out and about (and away from their computers). Explore the range of what mobile offers—such as offering a mobile app for your products or services. With today's smartphones, you're not limited to short text bursts or voice communications—today the medium lets you share information visually.

4. Celebrating Creativity with a Killer Smile: Creating a Viral Marketing Effect with an Online Game

Oscar Wilde said, "One should either be a work of art, or wear a work of art." The creators of this online visual marketing promotion combined Wilde's two options, allowing people to express their creativity by becoming a masterpiece. MasterpieceYourself.com is a game where everyone wins. Simply insert your portrait into a masterpiece by a famous artist like van Gogh or Michelangelo. And publish it. You may resize it, rotate it, name your portrait, and send it to a friend by e-mail or by posting it on Facebook. More than 100,000 people have played the game.

Cool van Gogh

With A Pearl Earring

MasterpieceYourself.com was created to promote the services of Langton Cherubino Group. They built buzz by using social networking services, including Facebook, Twitter, and LinkedIn, and creating a viral marketing campaign by contacting bloggers, websites, and publications. Spread by word of mouth online, soon traffic to the game doubled many times over.

Why It Works

More than half of the implementation time was spent on the interface design and navigation. "We wanted it to be fast and easy-to-use," says designer Jim Keller. From the design standpoint, this means you have to think about how users will move around the site. You need to determine where instructions are needed and where users may simply click and act.

Success Metrics

- MasterpieceYourself.com was featured in *Redbook* magazine.
- It has also been featured on radio stations and blogs, including as a learning tool, and has gained an audience worldwide.
- The site won the 2009 American Web Design Award from *Graphic Design USA* magazine.
- MasterpieceYourself.com has been identified by several prospective clients as the reason they became aware of or chose the Langton Cherubino Group for their online design needs.

Takeaway Tip

Create an interactive online game to generate a viral effect (meaning that something is spread by others) that pumps up the impact of your marketing. To be effective the game must be so visually and intellectually engaging and intriguing that people can't help but share it with others. It amplifies your marketing—word of mouth will kick in to spread the message for you. Make it (1) interesting to your target audience, (2) relevant to your business or core competencies, and (3) intuitive and simple enough for people to dive right in and "get it" without extensive instructions.

5. Putting the "Self" in Self-Portrait: Finding the Right Photo to Express a Personal Brand

The standard head shot may be safe, but it can be boring. Michelle Villalobos found this out when she selected the right image to represent herself and her personal brand. Villalobos runs workshops and teaches marketing and business concepts to professionals. Her most popular program is You: *The (Online) Brand*. She often uses multicolored Sharpie markers to draw charts and liven up her visual presentations. She knows the value of using the right image to make a point in education and promotion.

Yet when it came to promoting herself on her blog, Facebook, LinkedIn, and Twitter accounts, she did what many professionals do: pose for traditional portraits in business attire. The result was a beautiful professional portrait—but it didn't really represent her. At one of her workshops on personal branding an audience member commented, "Your portrait doesn't reflect your brand—you're fun, young and vibrant, your headshot is sedate and boring.

It's beautiful, but it looks like it belongs on Match.com—it's not the *you* we met today."

Why It Works

Villalobos decided to practice what she preaches and selected a photo of herself that emphasized her creative side. Fortunately, during the photo sessions with photographer Gio Alma she was warming up with her trade tool of choice, a handful of Sharpie markers. She initially dismissed these photos, "I thought the Sharpie pics were silly, *obviously* not something I would use professionally," says Villalobos with a chuckle. And yet, she realized that they captured the side of her that resonated with clients. Villalobos says, "I'm blown away by how much my headshot has done to boost my business online . . .

People make judgments about you *within the first 3 seconds* of meeting you." Villalobos adds, that she finds most people are much more comfortable working with a person rather than a business. "The Sharpie picture was the catalyst that has made my image the personal brand for my company." Villalobos changed her URL from MivistaConsulting.com, her business name, to MichelleVillalobos.com to reflect her personal brand, and she now receives 45 percent of her new business leads from Google searches.

Success Metrics

- Since embracing the Michelle Villalobos personal brand and the "Sharpie Girl" portrait, Villalobos has added 15 new corporate clients, including Burger King, Everglades National Park, LexisNexis, and Constant Contact.
- Villalobos's mailing list has grown from 2,500 names to more than 9,500.
- In the past year, revenues have nearly tripled.

Takeaway Tip

When you are selling *you* (i.e., your services as a consultant or other professional), then having a standout photograph is crucial for marketing online. A little creativity can transform a plain vanilla head shot into one that people will remember based on the pose, facial expression, or props you use. Make your photograph a friendly and accessible face for your personal brand. Clients and prospects will respond and will remember you.

6. Luxury Property Shown in Many Different Lights: Focusing on Stunning Imagery to Sell Luxury

What's the best time of day to see a luxury building? How do you capture the way the sun bounces off the Hudson River and illuminates the sculptural façade of a modern architectural jewel? The design team promoting 166 Perry Street, a luxury condominium project in New York City, decided to show how the building looks from daybreak to nightfall. Lilly Schonwald from Corcoran Sunshine Marketing Group says that the design is based on the light and air, how it relates back to nature and its surroundings, and how it changes during different time periods throughout the day.

The eight-story "jewel box" building with 24 residences was designed by the celebrated husband and wife team of Hani Rashid and Lise Anne Couture of Asymptote Architecture. Petter Ringbom of Flat Inc., an interactive design firm, worked in collaboration with Pentagram partner Michael Beirut to create visual marketing for the project that includes a website, property brochure, and presentation video.

Why It Works

When you are trying to sell a property before it is built, you need to work harder to capture the character of the space. This building caters to a very sophisticated clientele who are able to spend $1.95 million on a one-bedroom apartment or up to $24 million on a penthouse with a private pool. The website and the property brochure are really image-builders, not direct sales tools. People in this market are not clicking to buy online, but they are using the marketing materials as an important credibility check. Schonwald said that the content on this website is not really different from other luxury condos, "it's the design that was different."

Success Metrics

- Of the 24 luxury residential units, 22 have been sold in one of the most difficult real estate markets in New York City.
- The site won the design award STEP Best of the Web Annual.

Takeaway Tip

When selling luxury goods or property, three words describe it: "design, design, design." Keep the copy short. Focus on beautifully rendered images. A website for luxury items won't necessarily be different from other websites in how it's set up. But the emphasis will be different—on stunning high-quality images, without a lot of words.

7. How Many Ways Can You Destroy Your Printer? Going Viral with a YouTube Video Contest That Plays upon Customer Frustrations

Expert Laser Services held a contest. They received only a handful of entries, yet it propelled impressive sales in new business. The Destroy Your Printer contest invited disgruntled businesspeople to create videos showing creative ways to destroy their nonfunctioning printers, copiers, or fax machines and blow off steam at the same time. Using the company's blog, website, Twitter, Facebook, and LinkedIn, Expert Laser Services asked companies in the New England area to submit a short movie of employees destroying a piece of office equipment.

Why It Works

"I would get so frustrated with a malfunctioning copier or printer," says Nathan Dube, Expert Laser Services social media engineer. After doing a quick Twitter search, Dube found that many people felt the same way. They received videos of printers being tossed off buildings, hunted down in the woods, or being fed into a log splinter. It's not the number of entries that matters—it's the number of viewers and the publicity that the contest generated that counts. Dube made a promotional video that has been seen by more than 5,000 visitors on YouTube. "The bottom line is we gained new sales," says Michael Carpentier, the company's president, "and a cover story in *Recycler* magazine." Carpentier says that the contest

really resonated with clients, and it properly positions Expert Laser Services as a solution provider. The video capitalizes on the anger associated with printer failures. Since Expert Laser Services fixes printers, they can actually address the pain points of their clients.

Success Metrics

- Expert Laser Services attributes new business sales to the Destroy Your Printer contest. Website traffic boosts include more than 4,000 views of the user videos.

- *Recycler* magazine ran a cover story about the contest and the *New York Times* called Nathan.
- The promotional video on YouTube has had more than 5,000 viewers and continues to average 5 to 10 views per week.

Takeaway Tip

Contests, especially ones with user-submitted videos, can go viral if the subject matter is interesting enough. It's not the number of entries—but how well the contest "speaks" to your target audience. Focusing on user-generated videos expressing frustrations that most people have experienced and that lend themselves to funny interpretation is a way to engage not only the contestants but the broader target audience of the contest's product sponsor.

8. Making a Legal Case for Insider Jokes: Using Cartoons to Market to Your Target Audience

Lawyers are often the subject of jokes, so who would think that the best way to reach them might be through humor? CaseCentral, founded in San Francisco in 1994, provides cloud-based electronic discovery software solutions to law firms and corporations that are used in preparing the pre-trial phase of a lawsuit. CaseCentral distinguishes itself from much larger competition with weekly installments of "Case in Point" cartoons. By using clever visual humor that cuts through the clutter with inside industry jokes, the cartoons establish a unique voice and brand.

Tom Fishburne draws the witty cartoons, working with CaseCentral's chief marketing officer, Steve d'Alencon, who often provides the spark of an idea.

Fishburne and d'Alencon e-mail riffs back and forth as they develop each cartoon. They consider themselves comedy partners.

Why It Works

The insider jokes cultivate a social circle of those in-the-know. Jokes and references are not universal but, in fact, are very specific to the industry, with topical themes that relate to current events. By providing a platform for the industry humor, CaseCentral becomes the source for topical humor and positions itself as the knowledge center and go-to firm for industry perspective. They are vigilant about protecting the integrity of the cartoons. "We never use the cartoons to promote CaseCentral," adds d'Alencon, "or to bash the competition."

The response has been so positive that they now hold "caption

contests" to solicit entries from clients and prospects. The winner receives a framed cartoon with his or her winning quip. In its own way it serves as a marketing boon for CaseCentral. And how many companies can see their advertising tool framed on the wall of their prospects?

Success Metrics

- The cartoon was launched at a legal conference in Seattle with a couple hundred attendees. According to d'Alencon, it now has a weekly audience of more than 40,000 viewers.
- "Case in Point" is distributed through a multichannel approach, including posts on Facebook, Twitter, and Flickr; via

blog readership with RSS feeds; and through e-mail blasts.
- Requests come in daily for reproduction rights on blogs, websites, and books and for use in professional PowerPoint presentations. In response to demand, CaseCentral opened an online store on Café Press, where fans may purchase custom prints and order cartoons on coffee mugs, T-shirts, and other merchandise.

Takeaway Tip

Don't be afraid to use humor and cartoons to build a distinctive brand. For business-to-business firms, especially those where it may seem hard to differentiate and stand out from competitors with larger marketing budgets, it can be just the point of difference you need.

9. Changing the Script on Scriptwriting: Organizing a Virtual Community Around an Event to Maximize Participation

Script Frenzy is a one-month writing blitz that takes place in April every year. The keys are the deadline—one month of writing—and the encouragement gained from the online community of writers. Volunteer chapters in 100 cities across the world organize kickoff parties, laptop meetings in coffee shops, and staged readings of completed scripts. Founder and executive director, Chris Baty, says that combining a deadline with encouragement and an online community can create miracles. Script Frenzy started in 2004 as an outgrowth of the National Novel Writing month that was launched in 1999 and grew to more than 70,000 participants in 50 countries. After seven years a formal structure was needed, so a nonprofit organization called the Office of Letters and Light was established.

Script Frenzy is their initiative dedicated to scriptwriting. "The idea is that if you love movies, then write one," says Baty.

Why It Works

Many budding writers love the idea of writing for the movies or television but get bogged down because they are not familiar with what a script should look like. Script Frenzy provides the format for scriptwriting and gets writers thinking in traditional scriptwriting terms. The online forums and e-mail communication from volunteer coordinators spur on the participants. "We think of it as a grassroots nudge," says Baty.

The Script Frenzy site has a Plot Machine that combats writer's block. With each click the game reveals a random combination of plot, characters, and scenarios that are intended to be absurd and zany. To win at Script Frenzy, writers sign up online and complete the goal of writing 100 pages in the month of April. Winners gain a Script Frenzy certificate, Web icon, and eternal bragging rights.

The Script Frenzy logo, created by Todd Blank, is the visual centerpiece for the organization. It captures old-time movie house grandeur—you can almost smell the popcorn—while using a brash and kinetic typeface that evokes the thrill of going out to the theater.

Success Metrics

- Participation in Script Frenzy has tripled since its inception five years ago, with more than 21,000 writers participating in 2010.
- A Young Writers program grew from 50 participants to 2,850 in three years.
- A total of 373,906 words were logged in the most recent Script Frenzy competition.

Takeaway Tip

Create a virtual community to whip up enthusiasm for an initiative. Encourage participation by making people feel like they are part of an important and exciting event, through cohesive visual elements around one central theme. Don't just slap up a website with some information about the initiative. Instead, immerse people in the event every time they set foot on the website. Every image and every page should make them feel like they are part of the initiative. Use interactive features to captivate attention and draw people back again and again to participate. This can work for a business initiative in your company, as well as a nonprofit initiative.

10. When Is a Cup of Tea More Than Just Another Cup? Stunning Photography on a Website Differentiates a Product

With luxurious photography as a backdrop, Two Leaves and a Bud Tea Company created a website design that conveys freshness, commitment to quality, and the uniqueness of the company's brand at a glance. They've managed to capture a sense of oneness with nature and convey social responsibility toward the environment and the small farmers who pick the tea. When you're selling a commodity, product differentiation is crucial. Yet, how do you differentiate something as timeless and ubiquitous as tea—something that can be bought in any grocery store and all over the Web?

How do you not only justify consumers paying a higher price for your product but develop brand loyalty that causes them to remember and seek out your product over the many other options out there?

Why It Works

The Two Leaves and a Bud Tea Company's website redesign uses a full background image that changes with each visit to the site. The images are the company's own photography and show the tea growing in lush green fields, the small farmers who tend the fields and pick the tea, tea in bowls, and other evocative images. Phil Edelstein, marketing director, says visitors to the website should experience, "a fresh journey each and every time."

"Most ecommerce experiences are so focused on selling efficiently and effectively that they forget about their brand. With our web redesign, we wanted to create an experience that didn't just sell and convert more users, but demonstrated our brand story and our immense passion for tea," says Edelstein.

Success Metrics

- The site conversion rate jumped 1 percent (from 3.5 percent to 4.5 percent) immediately upon launching the redesign. Growth continues.

- The company has received immensely positive feedback from consumers, the press, and our wholesale clients.
- Company staff has a sense of pride in the company.

Takeaway Tip

Make sure your photography is top-notch if you're planning to use it to create the perception of a premium product. Clear images, evocative subject matter, and stunning compositions are key. Dare to be different. Just because a typical e-commerce site has a plain background, doesn't mean you need to be bound by it. After all, if your product is different, your website should be, too. Stylish photography can celebrate your unique brand and turn a commodity into a distinctive must-have product.

11. Just the Facts, Ma'am: Creating an Interactive Online Quiz Attracts a Target Audience with a Deeper Level of Engagement

Is a "blook" a criminal or an online book? Does a detective need a "Search clause," or is that something Google would do? Play Web vs. Webb to find out if you can tell if a phrase is from the World Wide Web or something uttered by Jack Webb, the actor who played Sergeant Joe Friday on the old TV show *Dragnet*. Web vs. Webb is a vintage TV quiz show–style game that may be played online. How does this promote a design firm in New York City?

Creating online games for your firm's website may not sound like a marketing stunt, but when your business does something a little offbeat and completely removed from its core business in the hopes of drumming up attention, it may be just that.

Why It Works

Incorporating the classic design motif from the early days of television, the word game heightens the contrast of the two modes of communication and the two technologies. Web vs. Webb equals television vs. Internet. It gives perspective—what was vs. what is.

An interesting by-product of this project is that the audiences are split along generation lines, as baby boomers readily identify with the "Just the facts,

ma'am," signature lines from *Dragnet*, while younger generations do not seem to recognize this jargon at all.

Success Metrics

- This site won the American Design Web Award from *Graphic Design USA*.
- The real success is getting noticed by clients and establishing a connection between

creative services and online solutions.
- The site helped secure more work for the firm with interactive and video solutions projects.

Takeaway Tip

An interactive online game draws people in and brings them to your website, and once there, it can engage their interest with more impact than traditional content, such as articles and white papers. This technique can be used by a design or IT firm wanting to showcase its Web design talent, but the same technique can be adapted to other types of businesses. When you create an online quiz, make sure the quiz relates to your business and will be of interest to your target audience. Although an unrelated quiz might be amusing and attract a lot of visitors, it won't help your business in the long run if they're not the kind of website visitors who fall into your target audience.

12. Getting a Leg Up on the Competition: Gaining Media Visibility for an Arcane Industry Online, Through Puns and Fun on Your Website

Recycling 100,000 pounds of mannequins a year may not sound glamorous, but it's what differentiates Mannequin Madness from its competitors. The mannequin company rents and sells mannequins of all shapes and sizes to not only retailers but also trade shows, artists, students, and anyone in need of a "dummy." And what could be a very industry-based business has a surprisingly fresh and friendly face—through its website and the myriad of media coverage it has gained over the past 10-plus years.

"We use videos, blogs, and photographs (online and offline) to promote our business," says Judi Townsend, founder of Mannequin Madness.

Why It Works

Mannequin Madness's website is intriguing and appealing to the eye: Each section of the site is identified by a corresponding mannequin part (including the famous leg lamp from *A Christmas Story*). Videos from the company and CNN plead to be watched on the side of the home page.

Besides the appropriate use of bright colors and solid layout, the website (and blog) offers a plethora of information about mannequins and their history, how the company recycles its mannequins (something most of us didn't know was possible),

along with links to social media and Yelp reviews. It has all the elements of a great website.

The company really found its niche by going beyond the traditional supplying to retailers. Trade shows often need mannequins for a conference, and buying them can be too costly for budgets. Artists want mannequins for art projects, and museums and theatrical productions also have the occasional need for a mannequin. By expanding its target audience and offering rentals, Mannequin Madness found the formula for success.

Success Metrics

- The company's recycling efforts have landed it contracts with Gap, Bebe, Nike, and Kohl's.
- Videos about the company have appeared on CNN, on the in-flight entertainment on British Airways flights, on TV shows about niche businesses and green businesses, as well as on YouTube.
- Flattering or not, Mannequin Madness has been so successful that its competitors are using its trademarked company name in their Google ads.

Takeaway Tip

No matter how arcane your industry or how boring you think your niche is, a website can take you from being technical and industrial to a business interest story the world wants to know about. Have fun with it. Use a tongue-in-cheek name and logo. Include visual jokes and puns. The media will pick up on it. It will be a powerful marketing tool.

13. Building an Appealing Design: Presenting Your Process in Your Website Showcases a Competitive Advantage for an Architectural Firm

For architecture firms, the proof is in the building, so to speak. Nothing markets a firm's services better than the buildings it has designed. Architectural Nexus wanted to display its portfolio on its website but also wanted to share its philosophies and process.

Brand design firm modern8 helped take the Architectural Nexus website beyond just a portfolio. While the Flash-based site features attractive photographs of the firm's work, it also speaks to who the firm is as an identity—something most architectural firms don't bother to do.

Why It Works

The firm's clients in the past, which included universities, health care groups, and religious organizations, had been spread across northern Utah, but the firm wanted to focus more tightly on regional projects.

We'd all like to pick our clients, but it can be difficult. Architectural Nexus found a way to do just that in how it presented itself through its site. Through its website redesign, Architectural Nexus was able to narrow in on the type of work it wanted more of, and it did so by illustrating its progressive, process-focused design approach.

The images alone are stunning, but the site goes further than just displaying pretty pictures of buildings. It uses a special section of the website to explain the firm's process for understanding and solving complex design problems, called "Problem Seeking." In this section, subtle clues reinforce that design is about uncovering and understanding, at a deep level, the client's vision for the project (for instance, the words "continue learning" are used instead of "read more" to advance to the next point).

Success Metrics

- The website won several awards, including a Utah Addy Awards 2011 Silver Addy Award and the Society for Marketing Professional Services Utah's 1st Place 2010 Electronic Professional award.
- The site looks and feels progressive, and the perceived value of the firm's services are greatly improved.

Takeaway Tip

If you are in a professional services business, keep your website simple, but do go beyond just a portfolio of your work. Share a bit of your company philosophy. If the way you handle projects is a competitive advantage, then outline your process. By understanding your vision before contacting you, potential clients will get a better feel for whether your style of working and theirs are consistent. And you will attract the kind of clients you prefer to work with.

14. A Visual Marketing Firm Uses Optical Illusions to See Things Differently: Showing Prospects What You Are Capable of in Multimedia

sound off

Have a cup of hot chocolate. Take a look out the window. Change the TV channel. See if you can solve the visual tricks in our Room of Illusions.

Langton Cherubino Group

119 West 23rd Street • Suite 700 • New York, NY 10011 • T 212.533.2585 • F 212.533.2448 • © Langton Cherubino Group, Ltd.

Chico Marx once said, "Who are you going to believe, me or your own eyes?" A design firm is really about seeing things differently. Jim Keller, design director at Langton Cherubino Group, always had a fondness for optical illusions such as the zigzag patterns that look crooked but are really straight or the paintings and etchings of Escher that play with your sense of perspective. Inspired by the visual tricks usually found on paper, the design team set off to create a Room of Illusions game that featured the classic optical puzzles online in a well-designed environment.

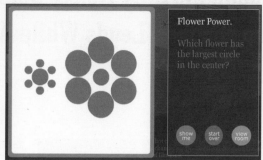
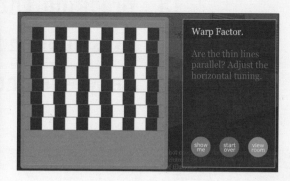

Why It Works

The tricks are as old as the printed page—yet in the hands of a designer, as fresh as today. The setting for the illusions is a futuristic room with bright color patterns featuring a Warner Brothers–era cartoon soundtrack. When you click on an item in the room, a large window opens and the illusion is presented as a challenge. The viewer tries to guess what the real truth is, and after another click, the secret is revealed. Each example is engaging and addictive. It's like when Penn and Teller show you how a trick works and lure you in for more mayhem. How did this come about? "Every year we like to send a New Year's card to our clients and friends," explains Jim. "This year we pushed ourselves to create something new with an old concept. We wanted to combine our visual wit with our online and interactive design capabilities."

Success Metrics

- The Room of Illusions game was the first of many self-promotional games that Langton Cherubino Group created. It established a method of combining design and programming that led to award-wining games such as MasterpieceYourself and Web vs. Webb.

- Clients responded and hired Langton Cherubino Group to create interactive games, including a series of "healthy games" for larger clients such as Pfizer and Publicis.

Takeaway Tip

Combine old-fashioned optical illusions with digital technology to create an interactive online game. For a design firm with multimedia expertise, it's an ideal way to showcase new media capabilities.

15. Breaking Through the Gray Noise: Using a Flash-Based Presentation to Generate Leads While Also Serving as a Leave-Behind Piece

In the public relations (PR) world, many try to put together a PowerPoint presentation to woo a potential client. But Gotham PR, a Manhattan-based PR firm specializing in fashion and design, asked itself how it could "break through the gray noise" in an industry filled with cookie-cutter pitches and presentations. The design firm The Art Department provided the answer: a four-minute Flash-based company overview incorporating fast-paced motion graphics and strong typography based on the concept "How Do You Break Through the Gray Noise?"

Five case studies are presented within the video, showcasing client successes and services. The movie CD itself has an appealing design and works well as a leave-behind. Gotham PR now uses the presentation not only in meetings but as a link from their website and embedded into blogs, Facebook, and Twitter feeds, according to Christie Grotheim of The Art Department.

Why It Works

Rather than making promises about what the firm will do for a potential customer, Gotham's presentation shows its experience, heavily based on event photos with celebrities and fashion designers. For those tired of PowerPoint slides, Gotham's video is a refreshing, upbeat change sure to energize any proposal meeting.

"The piece is multi-faceted, which is why it's been so successful," says Grotheim. "The challenge was that Gotham PR wanted something they could use in meetings for a dynamic presentation (beats PowerPoint!) that incorporated case studies, client lists, services and overview—a lot of information."

Success Metrics

- Gotham says that the Flash presentation is definitely a driver when working in an increasingly "visual" marketplace and global media.
- The video has proved to be a great display and recruitment tool, both client and team side.
- Gotham is receiving three to five qualified new business leads daily.

Takeaway Tip

Don't get stuck in the same rut as everyone else in your industry; it's boring. A bold, dynamic, and artistic Flash presentation can help you cut through the noise, showcase what you do, and get tongues wagging (in a good way) about you. More important, it can attract leads. Put it online and burn it to a disk for a leave-behind piece.

16. Delivering a Unique Marketing Campaign: Combining Staged Marketing Events with Video and Social Media

When's the last time you saw something that made you stop and gawk on the street? That's exactly what New Yorkers did when Delivery.com got their attention. The food delivery service sent two delivery men (Delivery Man Stan and Delivery Man Sam) with a *very large* delivery of food boxes, bags, and drinks to make a splash. They also passed out $5-off coupons to the onlookers. Everyone wanted to be a part of the experience: Tourists had photos taken with the two, others took their own photos and videos, and the pair even got advice from an onlooker not to spill anything. Talk about marketing interaction!

Why It Works

The campaign was well thought out and connected with other channels, such as YouTube, Facebook, and Twitter. The entire stunt was filmed to get people's reactions to the teetering pile of deliveries.

Delivery.com succeeded in moving marketing offline to real time, and then pushing it back to online. People love sharing a spectacle, and photos and videos of the street promotion were shared on social media sites. The delivery men were outgoing and played the silly role well.

The brand's social media play is strong as well: Delivery.com randomly picks a tweeter talking about the service and awards prizes and gift cards.

Success Metrics

- The campaign got people talking about Delivery.com on Twitter, Facebook, and YouTube. Thousands of people follow Delivery.com on the sites.
- From 5 to 6 percent of people who received gift cards on the street went online and used them. Delivery.com also held a citywide gift card handout after this campaign.
- Estimated return on investment (ROI) for the entire campaign, lasting several weeks, was a 15 to 20 percent increase of new users.

Takeaway Tip

Don't be afraid to do the outrageous. Staged marketing events and stunts work. In fact, sometimes the crazier it is, the more buzz it will get—just consider all angles so you don't offend important constituents, cause safety issues, or otherwise lead to negative publicity. And for the biggest bang for your buck today, tie in offline stunts with video and social media campaigns. That way the public can share the offline experience with others virtually online and through social media channels, and you will extend the reach and shelf life of your marketing stunt far longer.

17. Finding Your Identity: Standing Out from the Crowd with a Website That Lets Your Personality Show Through

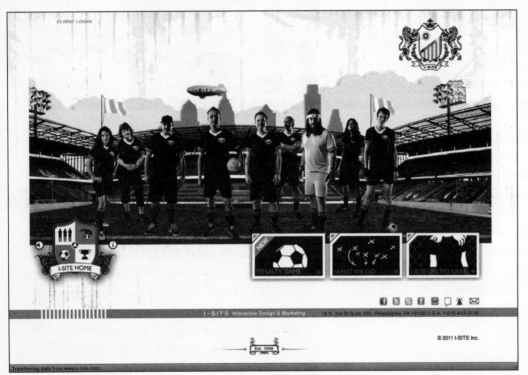

It's a catch-22: interactive media companies want to stand out from the crowd, but all their websites are the same boring thing. How can they strut their stuff if their sites look like cookie-cutter versions of their competitors? I-SITE refused to fall into this trap. The design agency wanted a website that expressed who they were through images and interaction, rather than through words. Ian Cross, chief executive officer of I-SITE, explains that the goal was "telling the I-SITE story—who we are, what we do, what we love in a highly visual and whimsical way."

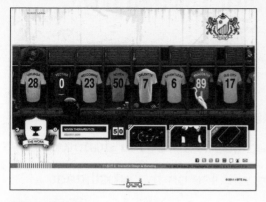

Why It Works

When you first visit I-SITE's page, you think it's for a soccer team . . . until you realize the motley crew is actually the staff of the agency. The entire site is built upon the concept of soccer—something that's obviously near and dear to the hearts of the staff. I-SITE even went so far as to create a soccer charity match complete with a cup for the winner. "If you're going to position yourself, you better play the game!" said Cross.

The site even sells beer steins and bottle openers (something else close to their hearts). The interactive and fun aspect of the site carries through to in-person marketing as well. I-SITE offers its unique beer coaster business cards—but only to those who they've invited to have a drink with them.

Success Metrics

- I-SITE's design has won numerous awards, including the American Design Award for Portfolio site.
- The new interactive design has improved the leads that come through the website.
- The site has also increased inquiries from designers and developers who want to work for I-SITE.

Takeaway Tip

Why do want your website and brand to look like every other business out there? To really stand out, represent who you are and who your company is, in all your unique glory. Letting your personality through and being yourself is what draws others to you. Although it may not resonate with everyone, remember that "everyone" is not your client base. Make it relevant to those you want to work with and who will appreciate your uniqueness.

18. A Renaissance for Today: Creating a Forward-Looking Logo That Reflects the Past

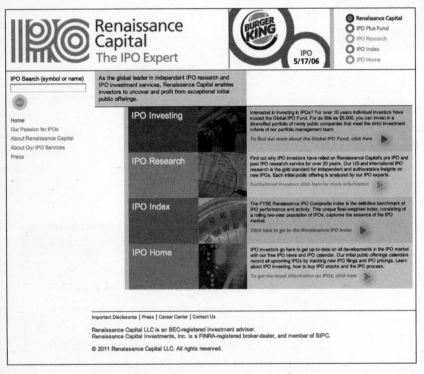

The original business card had "Renaissance Capital" spelled out in an Old English typeface—the kind you see on the mastheads of newspapers like the *New York Times*. It looked old, so it must be from the Renaissance, right? Turns out the design was just old. Kathleen Shelton Smith, William Smith, and Linda Killian, the founders of the Connecticut-based research firm Renaissance Capital, named their firm for the entrepreneurial spirit of innovation and invention embodied by da Vinci and Michelangelo. They believed that the founders of new companies like Google, eBay, and Facebook were the Renaissance people of today. After 15 years in business, the timing was right for Langton Cherubino Group to create a brand that supported the mission of the founders.

Why It Works

Shelton Smith insisted that the logo say "I-P-O," the financial shorthand for "initial public offering." They are IPO experts and are frequently quoted in the *Wall Street Journal* and seen on CNBC. But evoking the spirit of an IPO is an impossible task. "It's not a universal theme or concept like stability or trustworthiness that we could build a design around," says design director Jim Keller. So the design team sought to capture the themes of innovations and inventiveness while building upon the classical forms of Renaissance art and architecture. They explored Renaissance flags, fairs, buildings, inventions, and da Vinci drawings. "But the client insisted it read as 'IPO,'" says Keller. So they went back and pored over the letters "IPO" repeatedly. A

combination surfaced, representing an Ionic column from Greek revivalist architecture, and a new identity emerged. The logo had genuine Renaissance roots, and it actually said "IPO." Investing in IPOs is about discovering the future. Now Renaissance Capital has a forward-looking logo that pays tribute to the past.

Success Metrics

- The new brand caught the attention of the Financial Times

Stock Exchange (FTSE) and led to a partnership with the European company.
- The new website was redesigned and reorganized to emphasize the key sales offerings. This has increased research subscribers and attracted new investors to the IPO mutual fund.
- A new IPO app for the iPhone was launched and has gained 3,000 subscribers.

Takeaway Tip

Over the years a logo may come to give the wrong impression about your company. If your logo conveys an impression that is contrary to your firm's capabilities and how you want your market to think of your brand today—or if it just seems tired and old-fashioned—then it's time for a logo overhaul. A fresh choice of colors, design, tagline, and font can make a powerful difference, without having to change your brand name.

19. Good Service Is Earned: Making a Brand Statement and Creating Viral Content Through Infographics

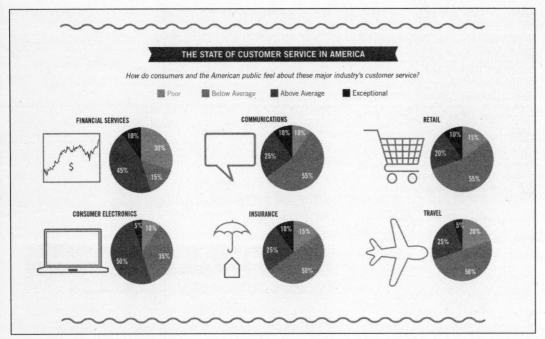

THE STATE OF CUSTOMER SERVICE IN AMERICA

How do consumers and the American public feel about these major industry's customer service?

■ Poor ■ Below Average ■ Above Average ■ Exceptional

FINANCIAL SERVICES
10% 30% 15% 45% 10%

COMMUNICATIONS
10% 10% 25% 55%

RETAIL
10% 15% 20% 55%

CONSUMER ELECTRONICS
5% 10% 35% 50%

INSURANCE
10% 15% 25% 50%

TRAVEL
5% 20% 25% 50%

Everybody knows good service when they experience it. And when they think customer service is bad, they talk about it. Openly. Social media brings new opportunities and increases the challenges for businesses that strive to deliver the best customer experiences—because people today talk freely online on social media sites. Get Satisfaction taps into crowdsourcing with a product that is part online forum and part social network to create a people-powered feedback that helps companies boost customer service. They spread the gospel of good customer service with striking infographics.

Why It Works

Infographics are like online posters with charts and statistics presented in a visual layout. They are a popular form of presenting information today. For Get Satisfaction, Column Five Media created an elaborate primer beginning with "The 10 Commandments of Good Customer Service" with colorful pie charts and symbols that visually explain the "State of Customer Service in America" and display rankings of the best—and worst—customer service in America. Keith Messick, vice president of marketing at Get Satisfaction says, "Our infographics are a crucial part of our content strategy in driving traffic to our site, generating leads and communicating our brand voice to the marketplace."

Success Metrics

- The Get Satisfaction blog has seen an increase in traffic of 3,000 percent since it started publishing infographics.
- More than 48,000 companies use Get Satisfaction to provide a more social support experience, build better products, increase search engine optimization (SEO), and improve customer loyalty.
- The Get Satisfaction infographics are retweeted every week, providing an ongoing conversation for the company and its services.

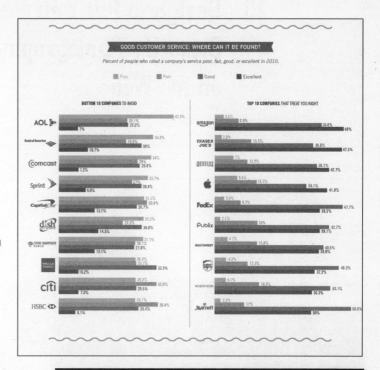

Takeaway Tip

Create infographics as part of the online content strategy for your business. Well-done infographics allow businesses to communicate powerful brand stories through compelling graphics. The best infographics have an element of entertainment to them, and people tend to share infographics—when they might not share the same information presented as text.

20. Design to Put Your Best Foot Forward: Using Sharp, Detailed Close-Up Photography to Demonstrate Business Capabilities on the Web

SCHWILLIAMZ

About Portfolio Process Clients Contact

Schwilliamz Creative Consultants, Inc. is a dynamic design firm that assists forward thinking clients with the design, development, and marketing of exceptional footwear. From idea generation to intelligence gathering to innovative design, our approach is thorough and fresh, and aimed squarely at one goal: to help our clients excel in the marketplace.

more +

News: Schwilliamz opens new office and hires new designer

The growth of a company is a good thing, but when your brand identity doesn't match where you're headed, it's time to call in the experts. That's what Schwilliamz Creative Consultants did when it felt its footwear design firm was looked upon more as a freelancing firm than a consultancy experienced (and successful) with taking entire lines from concept through manufacturing. "To establish and grow Schwilliamz, we initially relied on existing business contacts and cold calls," says Dean Schwartz, principal of Schwilliamz.

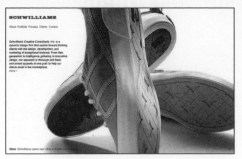

"As our business grew and matured, we recognized the need for a more focused and professional marketing plan. We determined that a website would be a vital component in our overall marketing and brand identity strategy."

Visual Dialogue saw immediately what Schwilliamz needed to make its brand look more professional online.

Why It Works

The resulting Web design puts Schwilliamz' stunning results front and center: from kid's sport shoes to high-fashion trend wear, the site displays the breadth and depth of the company's work. Descriptive text, press coverage, and background information go beyond the finished design to show potential clients their process and the end results in the marketplace.

A rotating series of shoe images—life-size, almost life-size, or sometimes larger than life—appear on every page of the site. Through the sharp photography, site visitors can examine every stitch and detail. It's a visual example of the company's portfolio—almost like a slideshow of their portfolio, only one doesn't need to sit through a presentation to see it.

Success Metrics

- Schwilliamz has expanded its sales in the United States and globally with clients in China.

- Schwilliamz' designs result in more than 3 million pairs of footwear annually.
- The design has helped change the perception of the consultancy and helped distinguish it from the competition—a true consultancy/business partner versus merely freelance designers.

Takeaway Tip

Instead of telling people what you can produce, show them! Put your output front and center on your website. Nothing says that you must limit your work product to a specific section dubbed "portfolio." But when photographs of what you produce become the focal point on every page, the quality of the images is paramount. They must be sharp, detailed, and close-up enough to invite and withstand scrutiny.

21. Spicing Up the Ornament Market: Using Bright and Unique Online Ads to Build a Brand

The holiday ornament market is one that most people think of for only about one month a year. That's not the case for Darlene Tenes, who, in 2007, was frustrated that she couldn't find any ornaments that reflected her Latino roots. Instead, she made her own. She now sells glassblown Sancho Snowmen, Day of the Dead skeletons, Hispanic pastries, and Frida Kahlos through her company. CasaQ essentially created the Hispanic ornament market on its own, due, in part, to Tenes's zany online marketing and direct-mail campaigns.

Why It Works

CasaQ's online ads are well designed, and although aimed at the Latino market, they appeal to a wider audience of people looking for unique ornaments. The elements of the ads include newspaper clippings, vintage images of women, and Technicolor photos of the ornaments, along with humorous messaging.

The ads are not traditional banner ads with slick graphics. Instead, the ads sometimes look like hand-drawn documents. One ad looks like doodles on a scratch pad with a hand-drawn design of an ornament, along with the company domain name in a script font as if it's handwritten. The CasaQ ornament that resulted from

the sketch "sits" on the scratch pad like a paperweight effect— and clearly identifies what the ad is about.

Takeaway Tip

It's possible to build a brand with online ads, without ever turning to print ads. All it takes is creativity, eye-catching color, and pizzazz.

Success Metrics

- After distributing its first press release, CasaQ was contacted by the Latin Grammy Awards to be featured in its official celebrity gift baskets.
- CasaQ's 17 different ornaments are now sold in Macy's and 70 museum and specialty shops across the nation.

22. A Reflection of Style: Incorporating Your Business Style into Your Logo

There are many small businesses that reflect their owners' personalities. Take Sarah Petty's The Joy of Marketing, for example. The owner and the business are so close, it made sense to design a logo that reflected her bright and playful style. As a successful photographer, Petty wanted to tie her photography business to a boutique marketing agency that could help creative business owners create a strong brand and profitable business. She also wanted a logo that fit in with its sister photography firm.

Marketing Caffeine for your Small Business

Why It Works

The Joy of Marketing logo feels joyful—giving extra meaning to the brand name "The Joy of Marketing." Petty wanted her marketing logo to be as bright and playful as her photography was. For different online events, The Joy of Marketing uses a slight variation of the logo to reflect different themes, which keeps the company's creative audience engaged. Another positive feature of the logo design is that it doesn't try to appeal to too wide an audience.

"We knew that because of the attention to detail we preached and the type of person who cares about those details, our audience would skew female," explained Petty. "We are large believers that as a business, you

don't want to be all things to all people. While we do have quite a few men in our audience, we definitely skew toward a female demographic."

Success Metrics

- Since the company's launch in 2005, it has grown to need a staff of five full-time employees and two part-time helpers.
- Its brand recognition within the photography industry is strong and continues to grow.

Takeaway Tip

There are plenty of impersonal logos out there—you need only look to the vast majority of corporate logos. As a small business you can afford to let your logo reflect your unique business style—especially when the logo incorporates the business owner's name. Think about whom your targeted audience consists of and play to them; don't go wider. For instance, if your target audience is predominantly female, then go for a logo with feminine touches and in feminine colors. Trying to stay with a neutral look and feel may make it only more difficult to appeal to your core audience.

23. The Right Way to Start a Charity Today: Using Facebook and Blogs to Build a Community Around a Good Cause

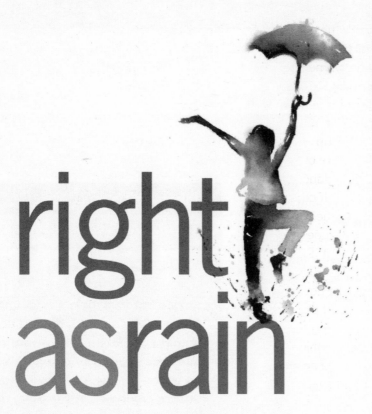

Sarah Dale doesn't consider herself to be an artist or a craftsperson, but when a friend needed financial assistance during a medical emergency, she created a series of gift cards and sold them to friends and family and raised $2,500. It worked so well that she and her husband, Gavino, decided to set up a Facebook page and a blog to encourage other artists and crafts people to join their crusade of "change the world one craft at a time."

Why It Works

Dale used Facebook and a blog that she created herself to spread the word about Right as Rain. She posts photos of the arts and crafts to promote sales. The organization focuses on one recipient at a time and uses the power of social networking to build a community of artisans and craftspeople to create the art and an ever-growing network of "rainmakers," who support the beneficiary by purchasing the artwork. Dale often reaches out to her network in online conversations seeking their advice and feedback on core issues such as who should be the next recipient as well as more rudimentary ones such as previewing videos and testing promotional methods. Dale has built an impressive network by effectively using these crowdsourcing techniques that engage her audience and improve the overall mission of Right as Rain. She tries to responds to every comment on Facebook herself.

The logo by Jim Keller at Langton Cherubino Group embraces the joie de vivre of Gene Kelly's exuberant dance from *Singin' in the Rain*. It captures the nonprofit's name and perfectly illustrates the hope and creativity that is instilled in Right as Rain. Rain can be destructive, or even just cause a bad day, but with an umbrella and playful attitude, the figure dancing on the logo has turned something negative into a happy moment.

Success Metrics

- Right as Rain built a network of more than 2,100 Facebook fans in less than two years.
- The charity has raised in excess of $15,000 and helped people in a variety of crises: from survivors of natural disasters to people fighting personal illness and injury. More than 300 people have made crafts and donated proceeds to Right as Rain.
- Right as Rain won the 2011 Communicator Award for Excellence in design.

Takeaway Tip

Use Facebook and blogs to engage your audience in back-and-forth dialogues about real issues and you will build a loyal base for your organization. When users contact you, be sure to give a personal response; this increases the engagement of your fans and supporters and ultimately builds up the community for your endeavor.

24. Education Can Be Creative: Formatting the Standard "10 Tips" Article to Convey Professionalism and Authority

TheHangline.com strives to educate people on effective billboard advertising. The new blog provided a great resource on the subject, but editors Todd Turner and Chad Hutchison wanted to go beyond the usual billboard advice ("use bright colors"). They then came up with a blog post called "The 10 Commandments of Outdoor Advertising." "Our article is written candidly and boldly," says art director Turner. "We call them commandments because people should not waiver from them. If you do, you fail."

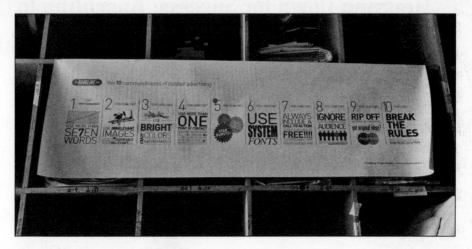

Why It Works

First, the tips are smart, and they include examples that broke the commandments, which are good for a laugh. "Thou Shalt Not Use Irrelevant Images" states: "Your dog doesn't belong on a billboard just because you think he's cute." Then it shows a billboard with not only a dog, but also two real estate agents. By using negative examples, the post gets its point across.

The post uses attractive decorative fonts and divider lines to make each tip easy to read. The post was so successful that TheHangline.com designed a poster of the commandments, available for sale on its site, as well as a free downloadable PDF.

The content was valuable enough to drive traffic and encourage people to share the post. The tie-in to the poster sale was effective in that it wasn't overbearing.

Success Metrics

- Before this article, the site averaged about 50 hits per day. After, it has experienced a 1,000 percent increase in subscribers.
- The site has had a 500 percent increase in daily traffic.
- The "10 Commandments" put TheHangline.com first in mind for people in the outdoor industry, with hundreds of mentions in social media.

Takeaway Tip

Love it or hate it, the "10 tips" article format is here to stay on blogs. But what sets apart a great example from a pedestrian one? Try a bold headline that establishes a theme and use attractive formatting for the article, including fonts, colors, headings, images, spacing, dividers, and more. Presentation is half the battle, and your job is not done once the article is written. You create a perception when you present an article—that perception can be authoritative or amateurish. It's up to you.

25. Dressing Down for Success: Appealing to Consumers with a Personal Video Demystifies a Confusing Subject and Builds Trust

At first glance, this site looks like just another corporate, professional insurance website, but then suddenly, a video shows a woman walking across the screen. Dressed in a bathrobe, she is wearing cold cream and carrying a laundry basket. This is how we meet State Farm insurance agent Deborah Becker. The biggest impression of the video is that dealing with the agent is fun and easy—and she starts by poking fun at herself. The video is engaging, personal, and fun—yet it manages to bring you back to the business matter at hand (i.e., dealing with your insurance needs).

Why It Works

Traditionally, insurance agents and financial service representatives have taken a staid and serious tone in communications with consumers. After all, insuring your home, auto, business, and other assets is very important to most of us. As Deborah Becker says, "We created the freedom for a back-and-forth comfortable exchange." Yet, the professionalism is there, and you get a sense that she as an agent still thinks the subject matter and nature of the visitor's interest is serious and important.

It differentiates her from other competing agents in her local area. Deborah says, "Our experience has shown that the average consumer does not really differentiate between the companies offering insurance products; they establish an emotional relationship with the icon that represents that company. We attempted to establish a "relationship history" between the consumer and Deborah Becker that would make the consumer feel as if they know, like, and therefore trust this individual to provide them with products and coverage that realistically fit their lifestyles."

Success Metrics

- The video has become such a viral sensation that Deborah has been able to eliminate all print, radio, and Yellow Pages advertising, and she now focuses solely on promoting the Web presence through online advertising. As a result, advertising costs were only one-fifth of the previous year's with increased business production. She became the most viewed State Farm agent in the country, despite being from a small market.
- The cost of the video was just $250, yet she has received thousands of e-mails congratulating her, expressing interest, and most important, asking to form a business relationship because of the video. "This advertising campaign was like hitting the Lotto!" says Deborah.

Takeaway Tip

Showing off your personality can add that needed touch of personal differentiation to a serious, professional-looking website. Add a personal video (recording of you or a company executive speaking). But the real power is in the details: Make it funny, yet keep it professional. Have the speaker "walk" across the website, making it seem more intimate.

26. A Legal Holiday: Using Electronic Greeting Cards to Position a Law Firm as Friendly

Manatt, Phelps & Phillips, LLP, is a law firm with offices across the United States, many legal talents, and an expert stable of qualified lawyers. It turns out that the firm also has a sense of humor. For the holiday season, the law firm retained Wechsler Ross & Partners to design an electronic holiday card that poked fun at itself and its professional peers and that positioned the firm as friendly and contemporary—no easy feat among lawyers.

Why It Works

This is likely one of very few amusing holiday cards from lawyers on the planet, which makes it even funnier. In the card, the lawyers go through the wording for their holiday card, but shoot down all options for fear of offending or inciting legal action. Finally the group settles on "warm wishes," which itself requires an asterisk to specify, among other things, that "the wish, whether warm, neutral or cold, is under no obligation to come true."

"Humor is a delicate area for a law firm, which must carefully avoid offense," says principal Dan Ross. Ross's objective in designing the e-card was to reinforce a warm relationship and inculcate positive feelings in an often-contentious profession.

The e-card was sent to clients, prospects, colleagues, and peers, as well as posted to its website, with resounding positive response.

Success Metrics

- The Manatt card was widely acclaimed in legal media and attracted extensive favorable publicity to the firm.
- An entire post was devoted to this card by the *Wall Street Journal's* Law Blog, which named it "the best law firm holiday card of 2010."

Takeaway Tip

Don't take yourself or your brand too seriously, especially if everyone else does. Stepping outside your traditional role and impression of gravitas for a special occasion like a holiday can make people smile and endear you to them. If done tastefully, you will not lose credibility. On the contrary, you just may gain a closer connection and bond of loyalty with clients.

27. A Picture Speaks a Thousand Words: Creating a Visual Interpretation of What You Do in an Industry Known for Facts and Figures

Market research firms aren't known for visual creativity: They tend to be all numbers and analysis. That's why Topic 101, a leading research firm with expertise in the college market, decided to make its site unlike any of its competitors. The company needed a site that reflected its positioning as not just another stuffy research firm, as well as one that spoke to its target audience of marketing directors, advertising agency creative directors, and graphic designers.

Why It Works

Topic 101 brought on Visual Dialogue for the task of visually interpreting who they were as a company. The design firm created a visual metaphor for the survey process used by Topic 101 by using evocative photos and videos that can be interpreted in different ways.

The design emphasized Topic 101's cutting-edge, relevant approach to research, which drives creative strategy (as opposed to competitors who just supply reams of data).

"Upon visiting the new site, potential clients' first reaction is 'I love your site!' This sets the tone for the whole partnership," says Susan Battista, president of Topic 101.

"The site now," Battista said, "tells Topic 101's story and conveys its point of differentiation in an interesting and thoughtful way."

Success Metrics

- Topic 101's client list has grown since the design and includes Dragon Software, Harvard Business School, MIT, and United Way.
- In 2010, billings went up 30 percent despite the recession.

- The rebrand helped Topic 101 become the leading strategic research firm in the New England market.

Takeaway Tip

Don't be defined by your industry. Decide what you want to be known for (even if it flies in the face of the traditionalists in your field) and use this to brand your company. Go against the grain to stand out. For example, if your industry is known for copious and detailed facts and figures, find a way to use visual elements to demonstrate your company's capabilities in simple terms.

28. Walking the Talk: Making a Website That Reflects the Principles Fundamental to Your Business

When your firm consists of innovation experts whose goal is to get client organizations to think differently and achieve creative breakthroughs, a dry and drab website does not aid your marketing efforts. A website should reflect the principles by which the business operates. You have to convey at a glance that you understand creativity and use it in your own business. That's why EdgeDweller turned to Citizen Studio to turn its website into something unique and unexpected. To draw the right kind of clients, the company had to express, through word and design, what it was capable of doing.

"EdgeDweller is all about challenging the norm and finding innovation in business," explained Linda Doherty of Citizen Studio.

The design team wanted to create imagery that was secondary and complementary to the copy on the site, which was, in Doherty's mind, spot on to the audience of C-level executives looking for a company to help take them to a new level through creative exploration.

Why It Works

The colors—shades of burnt reds, spring greens, and lemon yellows—are more reminiscent of a summer dress than a professional consulting website.

The typical consulting website is blue, filled with images of suited businesspeople in the top quadrant. When reviewing site after site in a row, there are only so many of those you can look at before your eyes cross. So it becomes a competitive advantage to have a website that is different, because it stands out and is memorable, compared with competitors' websites, which all tend to look the same.

Most important, the website reflects a distinct artistic touch, reminiscent of the creativity that EdgeDweller's work brings out in its clients, without being too "out there."

Success Metrics

- EdgeDweller has established itself as providing evolutionary thinking for companies such as Avon, General Electric, and Disney.
- Its team has developed a growing reputation as leadership experts worldwide.

Takeaway Tip

When your business is based on differentiating itself from competitors through its creativity, then it's important to reflect some of that creativity in your website. At the same time, if the prospects and clients you deal with are corporate people, then to resonate with them, the creativity has to take the form of subtle touches such as unexpected colors and images; refrain from being too over the top.

29. Traversing from Print to Mobile: Creating a Mobile App Version of Print for Customers with a Foot in the Mobile World

Meal Tickets & Unusual Ideas has been designing and marketing its "little card displays" in more than 70 hotels and wineries in Northwestern Michigan for nearly 10 years, but it recognized that it needed to have a mobile presence. The result: the Traverse Traveler iPhone app, which is a handy mobile guide to Traverse City, Michigan, and the surrounding area. Advertisers get both print and mobile media exposure for the same rate, and Meal Tickets & Unusual Ideas has been able to expand its clientele by including lodging properties, entertainment, services, and local events on the app.

"We are a small business promoting other small businesses. And we believe it's important to keep up with technology to meet our customers needs," says Brandy Wheeler of Meal Tickets & Unusual Ideas.

Why It Works

Like most travel apps, the core audience was initially visitors to Northwestern Michigan. But the app has a surprising secondary audience. Wheeler says, "We've found that locals love it because it's such a handy resource for contacting the businesses they visit regularly and discovering new ones."

By tying the app in to advertising opportunities for clients, Meal Tickets & Unusual Ideas has created increased value for customers, as well as a free, useful application for anyone in the area with an iPhone.

Success Metrics

- Despite launching the app just before the holidays—in freezing temperatures and during the slowest business time of the year—the app reached 1,000 downloads in the first 25 days.
- Local media picked up the story the day the press release went out, which resulted in two TV interviews, live radio interviews, and several print stories within days.
- Businesses in the area have not only signed up for the app but also promoted it via Facebook and Twitter.

Takeaway Tip

The state of transmitting and consuming information is changing with the explosive growth of technology. And it's not just transitioning online—we're already in the mobile age. Convert what you are doing today in print to mobile devices. Create a mobile app that mirrors the print version but is attuned to and takes advantage of the unique attributes of mobile media to bridge the divide between old-school print and new school mobile.

30. Promoting Logos with a Guess-That-Logo Contest: Tying in a Contest with E-Mail Marketing to Increase Client Engagement

E-mail is a critical component for Langton Cherubino Group's monthly marketing strategy. Each month the company sets out to inform, educate, and amuse clients and prospects with stories about design intelligence, inspiration, and interaction. To promote its new online portfolio of logos, the company created a Guess-That-Logo contest and spiked interest in the firm's branding design services.

Why It Works

"We deplore logo contests," says cofounder Norman Cherubino. "When designers are working for free and only the winner gets paid it sets up a terrible precedent." Langton Cherubino Group believes that the best way to design a new identity is to get to know the company and its target audience. Without access to the client, it's very hard to create an identity that captures the right personality and meets your objectives. The twist on this logo contest was that they did not seek logo submissions; they asked clients and prospects to guess which logo belonged to an East Village restaurant. To find out, participants need only go to the online Logo Portfolio and search the gallery for the answers—which is exactly what the design firm wanted people

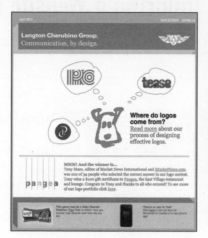

to do. The contest promoted one of their clients (a local restaurant) and offered a $100 gift certificate to a random winner.

Success Metrics

- The logo contest generated 48 votes from an e-mail list of 1,042 (a 4.6 percent return).
- The contest e-mail had an open rate of 27 percent, and the following month's e-mail announcing the winner had an open rate of 31 percent.
- The campaign increased Langton Cherubino Group's branding capabilities and led

to a new client meeting and an opportunity to bid on a major website redesign.

Takeaway Tip

Boost your e-mail marketing readership with a contest and gift certificate giveaway that generates interest in the products or services you offer. Contests can be effective ways to increase engagement with your target audience—they appeal to our sense of competitiveness and our curiosity. They can even allow you to toot your own horn graciously without appearing arrogant, as when an integral part of the contest invites people to look at your products or output.

31. Marketing to Parents: Tailoring a Website's Look to Reinforce Your Target Niche

Choosing a dentist for your child can be difficult without referrals. All you've really got to go on is a list of providers from your insurance company—or the phone book. How can you be sure the dentist will be good enough for your child? Seattle Kids Dentistry recognizes the importance of marketing to parents. Its website is filled with bright colors and images that will appeal to kids (should their parents decide to go over the site with them to make them feel at ease). It also is aimed at giving parents information about its dentists, office, and practice.

Why It Works

It's still (strangely) an oddity for any kind of doctor to have a well-designed website. Not only is this one visually appealing, it also puts parents' minds at ease with information about their child's first visit and what to expect. The element of education for parents is as important as the design.

The canary yellow theme, with accents of baby blue and white and a peppering of images of babies and kids, makes it clear that this dentist's office is intended for children. Other simple graphics make the site appealing and easy to navigate. Its "Did You Know" tidbits delight visitors with their intriguing tooth-related facts, such as "A knocked out tooth starts to die within 15 minutes, but if you put it in milk or hold it in your mouth it will survive longer."

Success Metrics

- Seattle Kids Dentistry's new brand and online presence has positioned the company to open two offices in the Seattle area.
- Because pediatric dentistry is a relatively new field, the firm has succeeded in branding itself in the field online.

Takeaway Tip

You've carefully defined your niche—now make sure you tailor your website just as carefully and specifically. Make the graphical elements, such as choice of colors and images, reinforce your specialty or market, especially if you are carving out a new niche. Don't forget the educational piece, either. Present content in an interesting fashion to teach your visitors what they want to know about your business.

32. Leading by Example: Using Stock Images in a Downloadable Tips Sheet to Demonstrate That Marketing Can Be Easy and Inexpensive

One path to higher customer sales is through providing educational resources, as e-mail marketing provider VerticalResponse well knows. Its free marketing guides, like "50 Ways to Grow Your Email List" are attractive and useful resources that educate business owners and funnel them into the sales cycle for the company. There's nothing worse than trying to shotgun a target too wide of an audience with a single product. But VerticalResponse recognizes that its users range from newbie marketers to seasoned professionals, so the company designs different level guides and tutorials to target each level.

19 Telemarketing
If you've got people on the phone, don't hang up until you ask if you can add them to your newsletter.

20 FishBowl
Put a fishbowl on your counter and hold a weekly prize giveaway - then announce it in your newsletter. Add everyone who put their card in to your newsletter list. Just make sure you have a sign that tells them they will be added to your email list.

VerticalResponse
www.verticalresponse.com

follow us on:
f t   4

50 WAYS TO GROW YOUR EMAIL LIST

26 Use a Video Contest
Host a contest where you have customers create a one-minute video about why they like your non-profit, your company or products. Ask your customers to send you the videos and post them on your Facebook page. Then have your visitors vote on which should win cash or prizes that you offer. Your contestants will email their lists, and post to Twitter and Facebook asking their friends to vote for them and you'll get more exposure. Count up the "likes" or comments on each video to determine the winner. Make sure you include an email opt-in form on your Facebook page to capture any email addresses.

VIDEO CONTEST

27 Handheld Devices
If you're at a tradeshow, at your store, spa, salon or restaurant, you can use handheld devices. With an iPhone or an Android you can use Bump Technologies' free app. You simply bump your phones together and instantly swap contact information. Sterizon has a specialized handheld device and application where your customers can type in their email address and it goes right into your VerticalResponse account. There is a monthly fee for that one, but it sounds cool!

Why It Works

"We have many small business owners as clients and we know that they are challenged for time since they have to 'wear a lot of hats' running their own business," says Kim Stiglitz, director of retention and conversion marketing at VerticalResponse. "We firmly believe that by creating simple, quick, and easy-to-use free guides, we can enable our clients to be more successful with their email, direct mail and postcard marketing."

The guides get right to the point with short tips. They use stock images for visual appeal, a fact that is deliberate, according to

Stiglitz. Rather than having 100 percent custom graphics, VerticalResponse uses stock images to lead by example and illustrate that marketing a business doesn't have to be hard or expensive.

Success Metrics

- VerticalResponse's guides have been downloaded 35,000 times in the past year alone.
- The "50 Ways to Grow Your Email List" guide was downloaded 2,500 times and is the third most popular guide in the past year.

Takeaway Tip

When creating downloadable content pieces, such as white papers, reports, or guides, make them visually appealing with stock images. While stock images aren't right for every situation, they can play a role to quickly and inexpensively add visual interest and break up large expanses of text, especially in "workhorse" pieces.

33. Blogger Outreach in the Cloud: Using a Visually Inspired Word Cloud to Start a Conversation with a Blogger

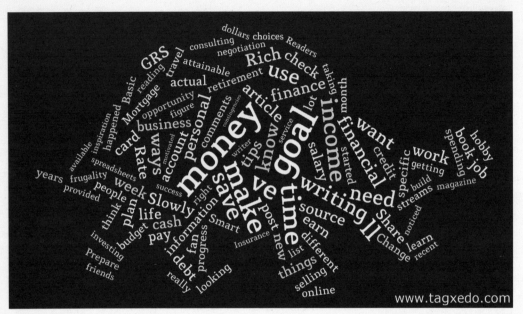

www.tagxedo.com

Getting bloggers to talk about your brand can be harder than pulling teeth: Your pitch tends to be like everyone else's, and bloggers simply aren't impressed. David de Souza, founder of TaxFix.co.uk, knew that getting the attention of money and finance bloggers would be a challenge, so he came up with an unusual idea. De Souza created a personalized word cloud in the shape of the logo from each blog on his outreach list and sent bloggers the logo-shaped word cloud along with a personal note. (A word cloud is a visual depiction of the main words used on a website or blog. The more often a word is used, the larger the size of the word.)

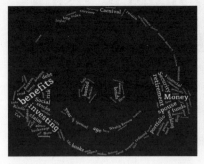

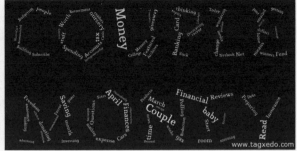

"The goal is to create a relationship with the blogger," de Souza explained. Once you've come to the blogger's attention, if you have quality content on your site the blogger may decide to write about it and link to it. "Links are like votes to the search engines and the more quality votes that you have . . . the more visitors."

Why It Works

De Souza did his homework. He identified the words each blogger used most frequently in his or her blog by analyzing the site content. Then he used a free online tool at Tagxedo.com that generated the word cloud in the shape of the blogger's logo. His aim—to make the word cloud interesting and personal to each blogger, so that they would share it with their readers—was true to its mark.

Imagine getting something completely personalized to you or your blog via e-mail. Naturally, you'd be intrigued, and chances are high that you'd want to share it with your blog readers. By taking this approach, de Souza got the attention of well-known finance bloggers and some very large and impressive websites.

Success Metrics

- One of the most popular finance blogs on the Web published de Souza's word cloud, giving his site a great boost in exposure.
- Thanks to the word cloud–driven outreach, TaxFix now ranks higher for a number of tax-related keywords.

34. An Illustrator Draws Up Timely Reminders for Prospects: Using Remarkable E-Mail Marketing to Keep Your Pipeline Full

Robert Pizzo captures the attention of busy art directors with his award-winning illustrations and continues to be one of the nation's busiest artists. It's not enough to be a talented artist; you must also be a good businessperson. Staying top of mind is not something you can take for granted. Pizzo uses e-mail marketing blasts with his artwork to stay visible.

Why It Works

Pizzo doesn't just repurpose existing artwork; he renders new illustrations that were created specifically for self-promotion. By creating original art for his own marketing, he shows off his thinking and creativity with each e-mail blast. The timing is also critical. He often whips up a timely promo that relates to special events such as daylight saving time. "They feel fresh and current, like little public service announcements," says Pizzo. There are rules for e-mailing that Pizzo adheres to: Always ask for permission, do not e-mail more than once a month, and keep the content simple—one image per e-mail is usually enough. Finding the right balance of content and timing is the key to success.

Success Metrics

- Pizzo has won awards from *Print*, *Graphis*, *How*, Desi, and AR100. His work appears in leading publications, including the *Wall Street Journal*, *BusinessWeek*, and *Newsweek*, among others.
- Pizzo measures his success by the fact that his e-mails keep him in contact with his clients, which means they'll keep thinking of him on a regular basis—even if it's six months to a year between assignments.
- Illustrators are freelancers who are used to feast or famine workloads. With e-mail marketing, Pizzo has been able to sustain long-term work sources and maintain a profitable workflow.

Takeaway Tip

People in your target market get bombarded daily by e-mails from prospective vendors. You must stay visible—and be distinctive—to stick out in a very crowded marketplace. Put together a regular schedule of e-mails to stay front and center with those you have permission to market to. Include the same level of attention to detail in your e-mails as you do in your products and services. And make whatever you deliver not just blah, but visually remarkable. Do that and you will have a steady pipeline of business.

35. Bringing the Topic of Skin Care to a Head: Messaging to Teens with a Clean Peppy Web Design

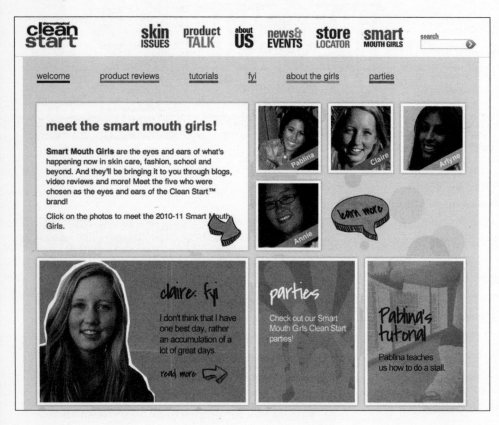

Marketing skin care products to teens can be as scary as a pre-prom zit. After all, the only people they listen to are other teens. That's the strategy Clean Start took in marketing its skin care line, a sub-brand of Dermalogica. Key is a bright and peppy Web look against a clean white background, provided by Hello Design.

Clean Start brought in the experts: five teenage girls dubbed the Smart Mouth Girls. The idea is that they share their skin care stories and their personalities through videos, social media, and blog posts and then other teens will respond and interact in Clean Start's community.

Why It Works

Teens don't want to be sold skin care products from adults. After all, adults just don't get it! But using the genuine voices of actual teens—not actors—gives this concept real teeth.

The website also offers practical advice on skin care, so the site becomes bigger than just e-commerce; it becomes a resource of information for teens looking to improve their skin. The clean look of the site reinforces the message that keeping skin clean and caring for your skin are important.

Success Metrics

- Since Clean Start's launch, visitor traffic increased 86 percent year over year and is steadily increasing.

- The more than 2,000 engaged fans that make up its active social media base constantly participate in conversations and share their experiences on Clean Start's Facebook page.
- The site has allowed Dermalogica to build and nurture a young audience to go beyond the hype in the skin care industry and really learn about and improve the health of their skin.

Takeaway Tip

Use design elements to reinforce your message. If your message is about keeping skin clean, for example, then a pristine look to your website and packaging will support that message.

36. It's Not All Business All the Time: Adding a Personalized Blog Header Brings Human Interest to a Business Website

Planning Startups Stories
Tim Berry on business planning, starting and growing your business, and having a life in the meantime

Entrepreneurs identify with their businesses, but there's always another side to them. Tim Berry, president and founder of Palo Alto Software, wanted to connect both his business and personal side in the design of his blog header that resides on a company website. Rodrigo Garcia helped Berry realize this effort in the blog header design that sits atop his business blog.

Since the business content—entrepreneurship and business planning—is well-represented in the blog itself, Berry decided to show a more casual unbusiness-like look. Berry says, "The banner would emphasize what's different about me."

Why It Works

Berry is a seasoned entrepreneur who is already well known in the business planning space, as is the company he founded and its products. By putting Berry out in front on the blog, it positions Berry as the public "face" of the company and humanizes it. His relaxed visage interjects a human element into an otherwise straightforward business site, creating greater customer intimacy.

There's a lot at play in this header. First the words describe what the blog is about. But the appealing nature scenes, combined with Berry's friendly face (a far cry from professional and stuffy head shots most of us have), put the reader at ease and tell us that this blog isn't just one more dry-as-dust company blog.

The stepping stones symbolize Berry's desire to make things easier for people by helping them through business planning, step by step. The mountains serve as a reminder that there's more to running a business than just working all the time. After all, what's the point of working hard if you can't play once in a while?

Success Metrics

- Berry shares his blog posts on Twitter and has been recommended as one of the top 20 entrepreneurs to follow on Twitter in *BusinessWeek* and one of 25 entrepreneurs to follow in *Business Insider*.
- He has been quoted and referenced in the *New York Times* and the *Wall Street Journal* as an expert, giving greater visibility to the company.

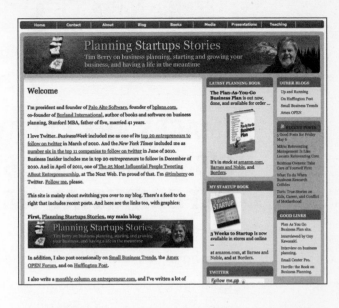

Takeaway Tip

Take some of the pressure off always focusing on work. Add an element of play and the human side into your design in a business-to-business industry. Your target audience will better identify with your company and products because of the personal touch—you create an emotional connection. A blog, with a simple personalized header, is a perfect place to interject the human element, but that same human touch can also work elsewhere.

Chapter 2

IMAGES ARE EVERYWHERE IN THE PHYSICAL WORLD: SIGNS, BANNERS, GIVEAWAYS, PACKAGING, AND EXPERIENTIAL MARKETING THAT INSPIRE AND PERSUADE

Visual marketing is all around you in the physical world. This chapter features projects you can hold in your hand, see on a billboard, or experience as you walk down the street. Among them are Rhode Island Community Bank's campaign for hunger, where they sold cans of "nothing" and raised thousands of dollars—and expanded their marketing visibility. Or there's DAAKE Design's "pillow talk" promotion, where they gave away pillows and then filmed a story of a lost pillow for anyone who didn't call them.

We can learn a lot from simple campaigns, like Lorden Oil company's "sock giveaway" that reminded people of the warmth and comfort of a well-heated home, to complex giveaways, like GGRP's cardboard record player that reaffirmed this recording studio as a player in the music biz. Tangible objects and stuff you see and touch in real life are all part of an effective visual marketing plan.

37. A Packaging Design That Really Helps the Consumer: Avoiding Lingo and Using Customers' Own Words to Stand Out

When the Beatles sing, "Help!" it is in full voice with an exclamation point. The makers of Help Remedies took a more soft-spoken approach. The Help home care medication products are designed in low-key white biodegradable packaging with bright colored trim and simple, elegant typography that clearly defines the task at hand: "help, I have a headache" or "help, I've cut myself." The design has caught the attention of consumers who want simple and effective pain relief from headaches, blisters, and aches and pains. "Too much in the healthcare aisle feels like doctors reading you lists of terrifying warnings," says company founder Richard Fine. "When you are sick that is the last thing you want: You want a friend to come over and be nice to you."

Why It Works

Consumers are looking for safe and trusted solutions to address common discomforts. Each Help Remedies product features only one all-natural active ingredient—no additives or coloring—and comes with straightforward directions. Packaging is bio-degradable, made of molded paper pulp and a bioplastic. The main idea behind Help Remedies is to make simple health issues simple. In doing so, they have created a visual format that supports the mission of the products they sell. The packaging and the language disdain marketing lingo and even avoid descriptions such as "extra strength," which the company thinks is superfluous.

Success Metrics

- Help Remedies has moved from selling products in high-end design stores (Virgin America, W Hotels & Resorts) into main-stream retailers such as Duane Reade and Target stores, result-ing in a 1,000 percent increase in distribution in about two years.
- The unique Help products story has had 80 million media impressions in a very traditional category.
- Help Remedies started with two prototypes. A year later they launched six products (head-ache, cut, blister, sleep, aching body, and allergy) and are now introducing two new categories.

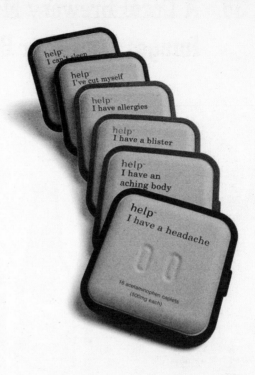

Takeaway Tip

Straight talk with a straightforward visual presentation can establish your product as a breakout leader in a cluttered marketplace. Avoid using lingo on your packaging. Instead, use words customers would use to describe the problem they want solved.

38. A Local Brewery Makes the Case for Better Beer Branding: Using Images from Your Business and Local Area to Brand Your Product

When the Colombia-based microbrewery Bogotá Beer Company (BBC) decided to redesign its identity, the solution was parked outside in the street. Their iconic Ford delivery truck became the central image for their brand and was included on the new labels for their line of beers. In Colombia, the SAB Miller Company dominates the beer market—they even own most of the local beers. BBC runs a small chain of 10 pubs and is the only local beer sold in convenience stores and in some major supermarkets.

Why It Works

BBC needed a distinctive design that celebrated Colombia. Each beer is named after a local Colombian neighborhood, and the names are boldly positioned on each label. The old Ford delivery truck appears in different angles so that each bottle has its own view of the truck. "We don't believe in design-based solutions. We believe in the thinking-based solutions," says creative director Lucho Correa of Lip, Ltda. At first Correa and designer Viviana Flórez created some pretty label designs, but Correa admits that they were just designs without much soul. They began working with the old truck images and thought about the posters announcing the wrestling and bullfighting events that resonate with the Bogotá urban scene.

According to Correa, the design just flowed. The design solution required a different approach with a more contemporary, yet classic look.

It's not just the beer labels—everything from the delivery boxes, to the glasses, to the signage support this reinvigorated brand. And many of the local shipments still arrive in an old Ford delivery truck.

Success Metrics

- Sales have more than doubled since the new packaging design was introduced. The regular 4-pack had to be replaced with a 6-pack to accommodate the increased beer sales.
- BBC packaging won the Communication Arts excellence in design award, and the Ibero American Design Biannual in

Madrid selected the labels for their show of the best design in Spain and Latin America.
- A special set of two bottles and a glass were created for the big French supermarket Carrefour, and it sold out in a few days.

Takeaway Tip

You may be able to find the key to your marketing success with an image that is right under your nose. Celebrate your connection with your local market by using images locals will recognize, including images from your own business (such as an image of a distinctive delivery truck that you use in the local community).

39. A New Spin on Making a Hit Record: Bringing Direct Mail Campaigns to the Next Level with a Mailer That Invites Recipients to Get "Hands-On"

Vinyl is the number one choice for audiophiles, so GGRP, a recording studio and music sound production company, decided to send out a 45 record to promote itself and make its case as the premier choice in quality sound engineering. Since few people have a record player handy these days, the creative team at Grey Vancouver created a mailer with a built-in needle and invented a cardboard album jacket that doubles as a record player.

Why It Works

The cardboard record player folds up to an envelope—or "record jacket"—that holds a vinyl 45 single with a children's story titled "A Town That Found Its Sound." The recording tells the GGRP story and reinforces how the company stands for creativity in sound and continues to deliver on quality for today's music and sound needs. The simplicity of the concept caught the attention of the company's target audience of creative directors across North America with a direct response exceeding 90 percent.

Success Metrics

- GGRP was inundated with requests for more cardboard record players.
- Gizmodo, the *Wall Street Journal*, *Wired*, and more than 500 blogs featured the cardboard record player on their blogs.
- Traffic to GGRP's website grew from 50 visits a week to more than 70,000 per week.
- The project won numerous awards, including the Gold at Cannes, as well as honors from the One Show and Marketing.

Takeaway Tip

Think about what your industry produces or represents professionally and come up with a hands-on kit that engages clients while reminding them of the products or services that can be found at your business. Although it takes more time to create a mailer like this, compared with the typical flat paper mailer, the results are exponentially better.

40. Making the Most of Your 15 Minutes of Fame: Using Posters and On-Site Displays Together with QR Codes and Social Media to Reach 24- to 45-Year-Olds

When the Andy Warhol exhibition came to the Anchorage Museum, Nerland Agency promoted the king of pop art on a shoestring budget. They created the Andy Warhol Factory Party to attract art patrons who usually disdain traditional marketing approaches.

Why It Works

The Nerland Agency consists of a couple of dozen employee-owners. Everyone who works there owns a piece of the agency. They joined with the local arts group, the International Gallery of Contemporary Art, to produce a Warhol Factory Party. They promoted it with large-format posters and pop art three-dimensional displays with bananas hanging on strings. The bananas were used in tribute to Warhol's Velvet Underground artwork. The eye-catching displays were hung at popular spots around town to build up publicity for the exhibition. The campaign used QR codes on all of the pieces. By scanning the codes with your smartphones, passersby could find out more party details and enter to win an original signed Warhol lithograph. The campaign was designed to reach 24- to 45-year-olds who are deeply immersed in mobile devices and social networking.

Success Factors

- The Warhol Factory Party event was sold out.
- The exhibition sold 13,000 tickets.
- NBC's Alaskan affiliate, KTUU-TV, featured the Warhol Factory Party on its website.

Takeaway Tip

To reach the 24- to 45-year-old demographic, don't rely on plain posters and on-site displays, no matter how beautiful and artistic. This demographic may find them lacking. Instead, incorporate the technology that infuses their daily lives, such as QR codes they can scan with their mobile devices to get additional information in digital form, and use integrated social media campaigns that make it easy for participants to readily share their real-world experiences with their friends virtually. Today this marriage of marketing, art, and technology is expected with younger demographics, and it makes for a richer experience.

41. Handing Your Brand Over to Your Customers: Getting Customers Deeply Engaged with Your Brand to Create Fanatical Loyalty

Sometimes the best thing you can do with your brand is give it away. Let your customers own it. Share it. Deliver it. That's what frozen yogurt shop Cuppa Yo did when opening its Bend, Oregon, storefront. The owners wanted a logo that would be immediately recognized and easily used in all areas of branding, especially because they planned to turn the yogurt shop into a franchise down the road. Design firm Studio Absolute created the attention-grabbing orange scalloped logo and put it to use on print ads, promotional items, signs, and the company's website. It also tied in fun messaging that helped the yogurt shop reach its demographic of young females, the "dating demographic," young families, and health-conscious individuals. "Satisfy Yo Craving," "Create Yo Masterpiece," and "Sweet on Yo Wallet" are just some examples of how Cuppa Yo took a fun approach with its marketing message.

Why It Works

Cuppa Yo's branding efforts began long before it opened its doors. It created not just a brand, but a culture that customers made their own through social media, bumper stickers, clothing, and community events.

Customers began to associate the orange logo and Cuppa Yo in general with happiness. After all, who doesn't love frozen yogurt?

Success Metrics

- Over the winter months, usually slow in this industry, the company averaged twice its initial projections for sales.
- After little over one year in business, Cuppa Yo has more than 5,400 active (near-fanatical) followers on Facebook.
- Due to its phenomenal success, Cuppa Yo opened a second location ahead of plan.

Takeaway Tip

Create a fun logo and brand identity that customers associate with happiness and pleasant things. Encourage them to get engaged with your brand through witty messaging that says the brand is about *them*. Customers will turn your brand into a culture by displaying your brand on bumper stickers, clothing, and elsewhere in the community. The result? Word of mouth and rabidly loyal customers.

42. Free Stuff for Dogs and the People Who Dig Them: Using Beautifully Designed Packaging for Free Product Samples "Sells" a Premium Product

about lani — dig your dog

Who'd have dreamed a silly dog could steal our hearts? But Lani did. Each beat and flutter. And, when she was gone, we found ourselves remembering every uniquely doggy moment. Her nuzzling up next to us on the sofa or greeting us at the door with her doggy dance, and us wrestling her into a bubbly tub after a good romp through the trees.

just add water, dog and stir.

How do you launch a premium dog shampoo? You give it away—in small doses. Peter O'Kuhn and Antonio Poglianich poured their hearts into a new organic pet grooming product line and stole a page from the beauty products playbook. They produced 10,000 mini-bottles and packets of lani dog shampoo and gave away free samples. "It engaged people," says O'Kuhn. "They smiled and were excited by the product." The combination of a winning design, a great product, and an inspirational story has established a premium brand that landed on the Valentine's Day segment of NBC's *Today* show.

Why It Works

The key was to spend as much time designing the samplers as they did the actual products. The samplers have the lani—dig your dog logo and a card that tells a story with a personal connection: just because it's a free giveaway doesn't mean it should look or feel cheap. In addition to creating a truly organic product, the lani team spent a great deal of time working with the Langton Cherubino Group to perfect the brand. O'Kuhn points out that once a great brand with a compelling story is established, there are many ways to promote it with social networking and online press services.

Their goal was to expand the category and promote the product outside the usual pet store channels. That's why in addition

to a host of pet publications, they are most proud of placements in *Real Simple*, *Coastal Living*, and *Southern Seasons*. A quarter of their sales are made online via the lani website, with the bulk of the sales being made through targeted retailers. The samplers have four primary uses: direct to consumers, business-to-business, charitable donations, and press promotion. "We've started a guerilla marketing campaign by giving away samples at the Chelsea dog park in our neighborhood," says O'Kuhn. Then lani expanded its efforts in dog parks all over Manhattan. Seeing how well the samplers worked one-on-one, they began giveaways in dog parks around the country, from Boston to Dallas and as far away as Puerto Rico.

Success Metrics

- Sales have increased each year by 10 to 20 percent.
- The lani products are now sold in more than 150 retail stores in the United States, Canada, Japan, and Europe.
- The design has won numerous awards, including the international Hermes Creative Award, which celebrates creative design.
- They have given away 10,000 samplers and are now preparing to place another order.

Takeaway Tip

Free does not mean cheap. Be sure to match the quality of your product in the promotional samples you give away. Pay as much attention to the design of your sample packaging as you do the packaging for the product itself, especially for luxury or premium products.

43. High-Tech Digital Communications from a 1970s Chevy Van: Marketing by Creating an "Experience" That Includes a Digital Billboard, Social Media, and an On-Site Presence

Would you spend a week living in a van in Indiana? In the bitter cold of winter? Broadcasting live via digital billboard and online? What if you could raise $18,000 for your favorite charity? Darren Heil, executive director of Community First Initiative (CFI), and Daniel Herndon, owner of Redwall Live, spent five days in an old 1970s Chevy van with nothing but a couple of bucket seats and an old couch. They braved temperatures in the low teens awaiting donors. Everything had to be donated: They wanted to spur on participation. "We had no food unless it was donated, no heat unless it was donated," says Herndon.

Why It Works

"The campaign is experiential, interactive and involves social media in a major way," explained Herndon. With a webcam and a couple of laptops, they blogged and tweeted as their image flickered 50 feet above on a billboard along Interstate 65 and streamed online via the Forkout.org website. Forkout.org is the charitable offspring of Redwall Live, an experiential marketing firm. They used social media to spread the news of the event and garnered attention from local press and from viewers online throughout the world. By living out this stunt and constantly communicating via Twitter, Facebook, and their blogs, Heil and Herndon created an urgency that encouraged people to donate. They created nine-minute webisodes that people could watch online as well as "a day in the life" videos. People could drive by and see the van and the digital images on the billboard. The combination of a live concept stunt with a digital billboard and the power of social media is what engaged viewers and ultimately persuaded donors to get involved.

Community First Initiative partners with local schools to provide specialized mentoring services for students. Even though the outdoor campout in the cold was unconventional, the attention-getting stunt actually reinforces the core mission of CFI of engaging the local community to work together in the growth and development of the next generation. Heil said that the interactive event allowed "[us to] stay in touch with people and create a personal connection between us and them during the five days."

Heil *told USA Today* that money has been harder to come by because of the struggling economy. They needed to do something different to capture the attention of potential donors. "It's worth doing whatever it takes to raise money," he added.

Success Metrics

- The Forkout for CFI raised $18,000.
- The campaign garnered great press coverage for CFI in local news, blogs, and an article published in *USA Today*.
- An estimated online audience of 150 to 1,500 tuned in each day during the event. A total of 175 donors contributed to the fund-raiser.

Takeaway Tip

Create a sense of urgency with a live daring stunt. Combine it with the power of social media (blogging and sharing the experience on social media sites) along with a roadside billboard to attract attention. The end result: You draw people into an "experience," and your message takes on deeper meaning and leads to action.

44. Designing Wine on the Inside . . . and Outside: Stimulating the Senses with High-End Packaging for a High-End Product

What happens when you combine the passions of a winemaker with visual designers? You get JAQK—Jack, Ace, Queen, and King—an exquisitely packaged wine bottle with a deck of distinctively designed playing cards. The visual marketing campaign for JAQK Cellars celebrates the passion for wine and the playful side of life.

Why It Works

Everything about JAQK Wines is carefully selected: from the grapes that Craig MacLean uses to produce the wine to the names like Pearl Handle and Her Majesty to the specialty glass from Milan to the design and marketing created by cofounders Katie Jain and Joel Templin of Hatch Design in San Francisco. They've combined wine and gaming in a classic high roller style. The trio indulged their love of wine and visual design to create a product that is well crafted on the inside . . . and on the outside.

Each wine is designed with its own motif and story. For example, 22 Black is named for the winning number Humphrey Bogart used in *Casablanca* when he let the young couple win at roulette. Jain points out that everybody plays cards, and for her wine company, she wanted a universal theme that would resonate with customers—not something that was about winemakers. The stories provide additional "talking points" for wine sellers and sommeliers, who, in addition to describing the vintage and character of the grapes, may share these tales with their customers.

Success Metrics

• Wine production has increased from 4,800 cases for the initial release to 8,000 for the second, and 11,000 cases are planned for the third release.

• JAQK wines are now distributed in 26 states and 9 countries.
• The San Francisco Museum of Modern Art acquired JAQK Cellars wines for their exhibition *How Wine Became Modern*. Hatch Design created all the accessories for the museum store, including wine coasters, canvas wine totes, and limited-edition lithograph posters of Napa, Sonoma, and other California wine regions.

Takeaway Tip

Make the packaging of your product as much a part of the sensory experience as the product itself. Appeal to the visual senses with artistic packaging that stimulates the brain and is a feast for the eyes. In a crowded field, it will make wholesalers and customers remember your product and give them a reason to single it out.

45. A Campaign That Really Knocks Your Socks Off: Appealing to Customers' Comfort Evokes Emotion and Differentiates a Commodity Business

The Lorden oil company found a way to get a leg up on the competition with its Knock Off Your Socks visual promotion. Images of extremely colorful socks in loud patterns adorn the company's oil trucks in an integrated campaign that featured print advertising, direct mail, telesales, and e-mail marketing promotions. As a family-owned and -operated business, Lorden has been delivering heating oil to homes in north central Massachusetts and southern New Hampshire for more than 70 years. Since consumers have low interest in changing their home heating provider, Todd Baird, vice president of strategy for Phillips Design Group, says he knew his company had to find the emotional connection to compel people to switch.

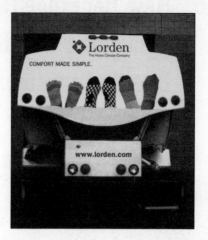

Why It Works

Homeowners who use oil to heat their homes tend to see fuel delivery as a commodity with little differentiation beyond price. The Lorden platform of "Comfort Made Simple" is expressed with playful sock images and Knock Your Socks Off promotional messaging. Lorden gave new and existing customers a pair of colorful socks. "This was the most successful promotion in the long history of our company. People were calling for socks," says Ted Lorden, president. "The free pair of socks really generated a ton of good will and increased retention for our business."

The big fuzzy socks mean warmth, and this campaign was a clever visual solution that supports the overall image of Lorden as a friendly, reliable family-owned business that connects with people in their homes in a personal way.

Success Metrics

- The Knock Your Socks Off campaign led to 300 new client accounts.
- The spirit of the program reinforced terrific word of mouth and built goodwill in the communities that Lorden serves.
- A local elementary school featured a "wear your Lorden socks" day.

Takeaway Tip

Pick images and promotional products that support the comfort of your customers. Appeal to their emotions if you want to make a commodity business stand out. Put the imagery that evokes emotion everywhere—signs, vehicles, advertisements, and online—to reinforce your message from many different vantage points.

46. New Beverage Design Creates Buzz: Simplicity in Packaging Emphasizes Purity in Ingredients for the Health-Conscious Market

After a bout with testicular cancer, David Luks listened to his nutritionist, who advised him to avoid artificial sweeteners. That inspired him to launch a line of healthy beverages. "I knew I wanted to do something with honey, a natural and common sweetener," says Luks. Honey has real health benefits, yet Luks was surprised to find that most brands actually used refined sugar to make their "honey" flavors. He learned that honey provides long-lasting energy because it is digested slowly in the body, whereas a refined sugar (such as white sugar or high-fructose corn syrup) actually spikes the blood sugar level in the body. Deluxe Honeydrop beverages are low-calorie drinks made with brewed tea and juices sweetened with a spoonful of real honey.

Why It Works

The Deluxe Honeydrop brand features a bold abstract bee—that also looks like a honey dipper (a wooden utensil with spiral grooves used for honey). Designer Mark Christou of Pearlfisher, who created the Honeydrop logo, says the logo "utilizes the honey-dipper bee icon as both a hero-symbol for honey and a clever rebus—or visual short hand." He says the iconic bee is a strong logo that can be seen alone on the front of a T-shirt or that can work in conjunction with the branding messages. The visual success relies on the simplicity of the design. The packaging features bold graphics, and by avoiding static studio photography, it conveys a natural freshness that connects with the health-conscious consumer. David Luks used his nickname, "D-Luks," in naming his new line of organic juices—Deluxe Honeydrop—and that alliteration helped inspire the branding messages that adorn each flavor: "Bee Good," "Bee Alive," "Bee Calm," and "Bee Strong."

Success Metrics

- Deluxe Honeydrop is now sold in more than 400 natural food retailers and co-ops, including 136 Whole Foods markets and 32 private yoga and Pilates studios.
- In one year, Deluxe Honeydrop sales grew an average of 27 percent per month.
- After its initial release, Deluxe Honeydrop became the number one selling beverage in the top Whole Foods store in New York City.

Takeaway Tip

When your product features truly natural ingredients (without fillers and artificial stuff) for the health-conscious consumer, your packaging must reflect the same level of purity to emphasize what's inside the product. A simple packaging design (without fillers and artificial stuff) resonates with this demographic.

47. Sustaining Good Design: Creating an Intentionally Retro Look Emphasizes Underlying Values

In 2008, the slow food movement was just beginning, and San Francisco was the epicenter of the development. The slow food movement emphasizes quality ingredients, often from local suppliers, and traditional healthiness of food, versus just eating quickly. The Slow Food Nation decided to host a three-day event in the city to celebrate and educate people about the slow food movement. The nonprofit retained Albertson Design to create a complete brand identity, website, advertising, print collateral, and signage for the event. According to David Albertson of Albertson Design, the event was designed to "raise awareness, experience new tastes, and celebrate local small-production food purveyors." He wanted a design that would reflect that goal.

The result was a cohesive, retro look across all channels. Silhouettes of farmers and farm animals graced the brochures, tickets, and the website. The result was a feeling of community, of caring for this one-of-a-kind event.

Why It Works

Each piece of the project is art, in and of itself. "The general design approach was to be exuberant, not earnest," says Albertson. The design is one that won't end up in the trash can after the event, but framed and remembered.

Albertson Design used environmental design applications, keeping the actual production in line with the bigger picture of sustainability.

Success Metrics

- A total of 85,000 people came together for the Slow Food Nation event in San Francisco.
- More than 3,000 collaborators contributed to the event and more than 600 articles covered it in print and Web media.
- The event attracted a wide range of people, many of whom were not "foodies," just folks who love food and have an

interest in knowing more about what makes good food good.

Takeaway Tip

Event marketing doesn't have to end up in the trash. Appeal to people's emotions and minds by artistically designed promotional materials that emphasize the values being espoused at the event. For ongoing branding, make the designs works of art that people will retain after the event is past.

48. Hand-Drawn Promo Excites Young Brits Who Love to Draw: Giving Away a High-Quality Gift Increases Sales by Luring People into the Store

Hey, do your kids know that they can actually draw without a handheld computer tablet? Cass Art celebrates the art of drawing and encourages kids to have fun with painting and drawing in new activity books designed by Angus Hyland of Pentagram UK, which feature delicate hand-drawn typography by Marion Deuchars.

Why It Works

Cass Art has five stores in London, where they have given away more than 15,000 illustrated children's activity books in a quality carry-around bag that makes the gift truly desirable. "Everyone likes something that's free . . . and educational," says Mark Cass. The promotion builds loyalty and has boosted sales for a new line of children's art supplies.

The Young British Artist label emblazoned on the side of the bag works on two levels. For children, it's a call to be artists, and for their parents, it's a sly reference to a group of visual artists also known as the YBAs, who began exhibiting together in London in the late 1980s. Cass Art believes in the power of art and encourages artistic expression at an early age. "We often hear five-year-olds say, 'I love this place,'" says Cass. This campaign excited the young artists—and their parents—leading to increased sales as it strengthened customer loyalty.

Success Metrics

- More than 15,000 kits have been given to customers at five London area stores.
- Sales have grown 20 percent over the past three years.

- Mark Cass says that driving people into the stores is the real key: "Once you get into the shop, it's very hard not to fill your basket."

Takeaway Tip

Everyone loves something for free—especially if it taps into the passions of your customers and reinforces the philosophy of your business. For retail, giving away a quality gift that gets people into your store and that recipients treasure will grow sales. Once in the store, people will spend. And they will come back.

49. Sweet! Creating an Interactive Puzzle to Increase Booth Traffic at a Conference

BizSugar.com is a social media site for small-business personnel. To increase awareness and build a community, BizSugar became an exhibitor at selected small-business events. The site's logo is a sugar cube, a play on the name BizSugar. With the help of designer Sarah Sawaya of Sassafras Design Services and marketing strategist Ivana Taylor of DIYMarketers.com, both in Ohio, BizSugar created a series of collateral pieces and trade show identity items—including a pop-up banner and tote bags—extending the sugar theme.

One of the collateral pieces was a comparison puzzle that consisted of two almost-identical sugar packet images describing BizSugar, but with seven subtle differences among them. Each attendee at a conference received a puzzle sheet. The puzzle instructed those who found the seven differences to visit the BizSugar booth to claim a special prize.

Why It Works

The sugar packet imagery reinforces the domain name of the site, BizSugar.com. Giving attendees a puzzle, something to "do," increased the interest level in the collateral piece. More important, it got people to come to the booth to claim their special prize for spotting the differences. Once there, they were presented with a brief demo of the site and given more information.

The puzzle was easy enough to create, and the cost of printing it was affordable on a small-business budget.

Success Metrics

- The puzzle is challenging but solvable, so plenty of people visited the booth throughout the conferences to claim their prize (a tote bag that also had a sugar packet design on it). The puzzle resulted in an estimated 40 percent increase in booth traffic.
- The site has grown from a few thousand registered users to more than 200,000 in a little over 18 months.
- Site traffic is now significant enough to have attracted a Fortune 500 sponsor.

Takeaway Tip

Use a game or puzzle to drive foot traffic at a conference or trade show to your booth; this will give you an opportunity for deeper interaction with attendees. Make the puzzle relevant to your business, products, or services to further reinforce your brand with attendees.

50. Jump-Starting a New Package Design: Creating Quality Packaging Can Lead to Getting Carried by More Retailers

As an emergency jump-starting product found on the shelves of automotive stores, standing out in a sea of red and black, checkerboard flags, and lightning bolt–designed packaging proved difficult for StartMeUp. "Its previous packaging had amateurish graphics on a cheap cardboard box that made potential customers wonder if StartMeUp would really work when needed," said Fritz Klaetke of Visual Dialogue. Visual Dialogue was assigned the task of breathing new life into StartMeUp's packaging. What the design firm didn't expect to do was find out who the product was really aimed at.

Why It Works

You'd probably expect that the new packaging appealed specifically to the average macho man browsing his local auto supply store. Au contraire.

Klaetke said they discovered that although anyone who drives a car is worried about having to deal with a dead battery, it is women who tend to be less likely to want to hook up jumper cables or flag down strangers. The emergency jump starter is one you can keep in your glove compartment, and it charges your battery through the cigarette lighter. "Women like small and simple," he says.

So the end design leaned toward women, using bright colors, a clean look, "easy as 1-2-3" logo, and a plastic case to convey confidence that StartMeUp will be easy to use. Klaetke says the design went more Martha Stewart than NASCAR, but the look is one that appeals to both sexes.

Success Metrics

- The new package design helped get StartMeUp carried by major retail stores, most notably Walmart.
- By rebranding the StartMeUp emergency jump starter, including new logo, package, and product design, the company reestablished consumer confidence in the product.

Takeaway Tip

Key to effective packaging is knowing your target audience well and designing a style of packaging that will appeal to that audience. Attractive packaging that suggests a quality product inside can also entice key retailers to carry the product.

51. Rewarding Good Taste: Growing Your Customer Base Through a Clever Twenty-First Century Loyalty Program

Newport Avenue Market in Bend, Oregon, knows that foodies are a loyal bunch. That's why the independently owned grocery store has long had a loyalty rewards program. Problem was, no one was taking advantage of the archaic stamp-based program. Enter Every Idea Marketing, who modernized the loyalty program to a digital version and provided a marketing campaign that made it hip to earn cash back on purchases. The store launched the campaign with print ads, store signs, e-mail newsletters, Facebook, Twitter, check stand signs, floor graphics, radio promotions and giveaways, product tie-ins, and a new paper shopping bag design.

Why It Works

Loyalty programs can work, but in this day and age, shoppers are reluctant to add yet another loyalty card to their keychains or wallets. Newport Avenue Market's digital loyalty cards have a unique feature: the FOODe Flash Card uses RFID (radio-frequency identification) and bar codes to make it easy to get instant rewards in the store.

By tying in e-mail marketing, the customer is constantly presented with relevant specials (including Super Secret Sales), and results show that they are more likely to take advantage of these than are non-loyalty-based customers. In fact, an average of 50 to 70 percent of total purchases at these sales has come from FOODe Flash Card holders.

Success Metrics

- Overall, store sales increased 6.5 percent in one year.
- The FOODe Flash Card program had 9,468 cardholders, with an average of 861 sign-ups per month.
- Approximately 68 percent of Newport Avenue Market shoppers are FOODe Flash Card holders.

Takeaway Tip

With market penetration in the loyalty rewards area reaching all-time highs, you have to provide extra benefits to your customers and entice them to participate. A program that uses the latest technology to provide special benefits and clever branding that makes customers feel "hip" for using it increases brand loyalty exponentially.

52. A New Product Popping Up: Differentiating a Product in a Crowded Field Through Unique, Uncluttered Packaging

Parents are tired of the limited selection of healthy snacks available for their children—and the even fewer healthy products that they'll actually eat. That's why Louise George founded United Kingdom–based Peter Popple's Popcorn, an air-popped, all-natural popcorn. The packaging is what makes it fun. The brand was launched at the 2010 specialty fine food fair in London, with orders being received from both major retailers and smaller delis.

"Although we are new, sales are ramping up in independent retailers, delis and farm shops week on week," says George.

Why It Works

Peter Popple's Popcorn decided to go in a different direction from what other kids' snacks were doing in terms of packaging. The retro Peter Popple "P" character is whimsical and simple, just like the product. The packaging is clear, so consumers can see exactly what they're buying.

The phrase, "It's popalicious!" appears on the packaging and marketing materials and has been trademarked with the intention of building future brand recall.

Success Metrics

- Peter Popple's Popcorn website received 1,000 visits within six months of its relaunch.
- More than 5,000 packets of Peter Popple's Popcorn were sold in the first six months after its launch in October 2010.
- The new product has been covered by media, including London's *The Evening Standard* and various food blogs and has been the center of attention at local events.

Takeaway Tip

Entering a crowded market can be daunting. But if existing competitors have cluttered packaging, try a different approach. Use simple packaging with remarkable graphics and a memorable mascot character to stand out.

53. Too Big to Ignore and Too Personal to Discard: Using "Lumpy Mail" to Get Your Foot in the Door of the C Suite

How do you attract the attention of chief executive officers (CEOs) at the top Fortune 1000 companies? Traditional methods like cold calling and letter writing rarely work, and even with electronic outreach via e-mails and social networking—if you can get into the right networks—it is increasingly difficult to penetrate. Ken Edmundson of Sandler Training selected five prospects and hand delivered a large poster board (18 × 36 inches) with a personalized cartoon and a prototype business book cover that featured the CEO as the author. All five prospects agreed to meet with him.

Why It Works

Stu Heinecke is a cartoonist and founder of CartoonLink, Inc. a marketing company that uses cartoons to reach prospects. Heinecke calls this "contact campaigning" and says the key is creating targeted customized drawings and punch lines that feature the CEO in a personal way. These are not just generic cartoons. The large size and the personal messaging make them hard to ignore—and it's hard to throw away a cartoon when you are featured in it. Heinecke experimented with a number of formats, including framed prints with an accompanying letter—which worked quite well but required additional packaging and special handling. The preferred format is a large poster board about the size of a flat-screen TV with a

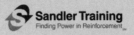

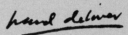

MAY I BRING YOU AN ADVANCE COPY OF YOUR BOOK, MR. FARACI?

Dear Mr. Faraci,

Changing the sales culture of your company to that of an apex hunter is a story I'd like to talk about helping you write.

The Sandler Sales approach I teach is grounded in modern methodologies that break through the price clutter and create competitive advantages for your salespeople.

I would like 20 minutes of your time to have a CEO-to-CEO conversation about what my firm does. When we meet, I will present you with a copy of your new book. I want your opinion as to whether my sales methodology fits International Paper.

Ken Edmundson, CEO
Edmundson Northstar Institute/Sandler Training
901-766-4560

Mr. John Faraci
CEO
International Paper
6400 Poplar Avenue
Memphis, TN 38197

customized cartoon on the front and a personal message from the sender on the back. Some versions include a calendar, which increases the likelihood that the piece will be displayed for a year.

Success Metrics

- CartoonLink BigBoards were sent to five Fortune 1000 CEOs, and all five agreed to meet with the Sandler representative.

- Two of the CEOs signed up for training immediately, resulting in more than $50,000 in sales.

Takeaway Tip

Bulk flat-mail pieces are easy to discard. Senior decision makers are bombarded with them. But an unexpectedly large piece customized to the recipient will invite the attention of busy C-level executives, who are often unreachable by other means.

54. Showcasing Talented Women: Creating a Calendar with Distinctive Photography for Yearlong Marketing

Sterling Women is a group of women business professionals who get together to learn from one another, network, and make new contacts. When founder Kristina Bouweiri decided to create a calendar showcasing some of the group's members, she initially planned to pay for the printing herself and give the calendars away as gifts. But advertisers jumped at the opportunity to get in front of Sterling's powerful women. In the end, the calendar served as a marketing tool for the featured women, as well as an ad platform for advertisers, who helped underwrite the production costs of the calendar.

"It was a win-win for everyone," says Bouweiri, CEO of Reston Limousine (pictured with one of her firm's cars, representing the month of December).

Why It Works

The calendar is an appealing way to show each woman's strengths and achievements through visual interpretation, furthering the purposes of the networking group. Each businesswoman is photographed by photographer Teri Moy in an environment that relates to her work. The photographs are creatively staged and exquisitely rendered, making the calendar images miniature works of art. The calendar serves as a reminder throughout the year of the women and their businesses, as well as the advertisers who appear in the calendar.

Success Metrics

- Sterling Women gave away 800 calendars in part to promote the women's businesses. They sold 200. The project was profitable.
- Due to the success of the campaign, Sterling Women now plans to release a calendar each year.

Takeaway Tip

Customers, clients, and business partners will treasure a high-quality paper calendar with creative, interesting photographs. People relate to real live people, and seeing them on a calendar builds trust for your brand throughout the entire year.

55. Get Your Clients Talking about You: Custom Designing Promotional Giveaways Makes a Big Splash

We all know the power of word of mouth. But how do you actually get clients to start telling others and feeling vested in your business? Photographer Leah Remillet, who caters to mothers, wanted to use every opportunity she had to get her clients talking about her. Her two goals in anything she did in her business were that it serve as a marketing platform and that it make Mom's day more fabulous. She did this by showering her clients with unique and useful gifts.

Why It Works

"Mom's don't expect things to be for them, any mother will attest: we give, not take," says Remillet. She wanted to surprise her clients by giving them gifts they could use: reusable jute bags for delivering orders, 3 X 3 mini albums for purses, and custom iPhone cases featuring Remillet's work.

"I wanted to first exceed any expectations in such a way that [the client] was dying to talk about me and then surprise her with wonderful gifts and products that give her the tools to showcase my business," says Remillet.

These aren't your typical stress ball tchotchkes. These are items that get clients talking to their friends about Remillet's business. By making the client feel special, Remillet is effectively building her army of brand evangelists.

Success Metrics

- Having spent only $200 on advertising last year, Remillet received three clients from that campaign and the rest came from referrals.
- Clients often send her gifts to reciprocate the love.
- Remillet is typically booked in advance for four to six weeks.

Takeaway Tip

Clients are number one. Make them feel special and they'll refer more business your way. If you give promotional items, don't waste it on plastic novelties, but spend it instead on something your clients can actually use—and that acts as a speaking tool for your business.

56. Breaking the Cutesy Barrier: Creating an Urban Chic Niche in an Existing Market with Displays and Packaging

Millions of people are dog lovers, but some are turned off by the cutesy and childish accessories that are sold in the marketplace. Fuzzy Nation wanted to break through to people who would be drawn to its "urban chic" accessories and handbags centered on the canine. The company works with the Art Department to tell its story graphically. Its packaging, website, trade shows, and product are consistently edgy, with gritty backgrounds and clever copy lines with massive dog heads peeking over packages and around walls (of trade show booths).

Why It Works

In creating its line of doggie-centric high fashion, Fuzzy Nation has created a niche. Dog lovers aren't forced to wear cartoon Snoopy shirts and carry teenaged girls' purses to show their love of poodles and pets. The Art Department furthered the message by designing its funky dog bone cross logo and its borderline biker website. They've elevated loving dogs to a coolness factor of 10.

"Our goal is to make sure our packaging works well as point of purchase (POP) in the store from all angles, to keep it upscale and engaging—which we achieve by using lots of white space with punches of warm red and black," explained Christie Grotheim of the Art Department.

Success Metrics

- Fuzzy Nation has expanded to four licensees and is evaluating three more.
- The company has opened a showroom in New York City and is also located in Macy's.
- Web sales were double that of the previous year.

Takeaway Tip

Don't let what your competitors do define your product. Do your own thing, and you'll often unearth an entire target market that didn't exist before, for example, an "urban chic" niche for an existing product category. Just make sure that your entire branding message, including displays, is consistent with the target niche you've carved out. If your niche is upscale, every aspect of your packaging and presence needs to be upscale, too.

57. Waking Up Your Brand with a Little Pillow Talk: Creating a Follow-Up Campaign That Makes Prospects Laugh . . . and Buy

How do designers dream up these concepts? DAAKE created a bright orange pillow with emoticons for "happy" and "sad" and sent them to clients. They selected a pillow because they wanted to signify "comfort" and wanted to give away something that would be kept. As a follow-up, they produced a two-minute video adventure showing the pillow in cartoon hijinks that would make the Roadrunner jealous.

Why It Works

The orange pillow seems outrageous enough, and yet that's just the beginning. Feedback from recipients of the pillow gift has been ecstatic. Many clients wrote asking for an appointment; one added, "My pillow is safely on top of my credenza—otherwise the cat in our office would shred it!" DAAKE hand picked 100 key prospects and delivered the pillow in a package with a brochure that asked, "Who is DAAKE?" If a client or prospect did not respond to the pillow, DAAKE would send them an e-mail asking, "Where is your pillow?" then attach the video that shows the poor pillow being thrown into a dumpster, donated to Goodwill, or being tossed out of a window. The adventures of the pillow are told to the soundtrack of an old Tom

Jones song. The video promotion itself became the catalyst for DAAKE's prospects. Instead of broadcasting the video on YouTube, DAAKE decided to "narrowcast" the video and use it as a one-to-one marketing follow-up.

Success Metrics

- In the first iteration, 100 pillow gifts were sent out, leading to 20 client meetings and three new customers (so far).
- DAAKE met its goal of attracting the attention of 100 key prospects and already recouped

their expenses on the new sales the campaign generated.

Takeaway Tip

Johnny Carson made a career out of the comeback joke, the quip that followed when the big joke bombed. When you plan a prospecting campaign, be sure to put just as much time and thought into how you will follow up with each prospect. Creating a follow-up that's just as clever and appealing as the initial campaign will increase your sales conversions.

58. Food Trucks, Today's Eatery Trend: Creating Cravings by Using Typography on a Truck Wrap

Street food vendors are popping up on every corner of New York City and beyond, so Street Sweets knew it needed to think big for its brand identity. The gourmet goodie provider brought in Landers Miller Design to help the company think creatively. The design firm went a nonconventional route: Rather than use images to brand Street Sweets, the focus was on typography. Words like *crave* and *delectable* are wrapped around the turquoise truck, guaranteeing attention anywhere it goes.

"In this case, we created something very flexible which can be applied to just about any and every situation," says Rick Landers of Landers Miller Design. "It doesn't require additional investment for visual assets and in every case creates a bold, and very visible presence."

Why It Works

Food is very visual, and it would have been easy to coat the truck in high-definition photos of cookies and cakes or to add a cutesy cupcake drawing to the logo. But using words demands the attention of the eye. The stomach follows.

The concept came from the idea of a street map and the hand-painted façades of French patisseries that use typography as texture, which ties in nicely with the French pastries Street Sweets sells. The branding is now used on the website and in marketing collateral to maintain consistency.

Success Metrics

- Since its launch, Street Sweets has hosted private events for Saks Fifth Avenue, Food Network, CitiGroup, Lexus, and Nike.
- An increase in private events has led Street Sweets to offer custom co-branded trucks for events.

Takeaway Tip

A vehicle wrap transforms an ordinary vehicle into a mobile billboard for your business. To take full advantage of that opportunity for visibility, make it bold; make it stand out. A bright color and words so big they take the place of graphics will make a bold statement.

59. Get Me a Doctor, STAT: Using a Witty or Humorous T-Shirt to Interject Fun into How People Perceive Your Business

The American College of Emergency Physicians (ACEP) wanted to attract young talent to the emergency room (ER) field but wasn't sure how to do it. ER physicians work long hours, and the work isn't glamorous. So the ACEP brought in design firm ohTwentyone to come up with a promotional item that would appeal to younger doctors.

ohTwentyone turned to pop culture to find its ideas. After watching a video put out by the staff of an ER that consisted of a tongue-in-cheek ER rap, the designers came up with an ingenious idea: a T-shirt, styled to look like the band AC/DC's logo, but instead reading ER/DR.

Why It Works

The medical industry isn't one known for humor. With lawsuits and malpractice cases abounding, it can be difficult to find the fun in being a doctor. This shirt elevates the ER physician into a rock star, and who doesn't want that?

The shirt was actually initially rejected by the client's board of directors, but a rebellious marketing manager had 2,000 of them printed on the sly to take them to ACEP's annual convention. They gave away all 2,000 in a few hours, proving the reluctant directors wrong.

Success Metrics

- This promotion received media attention from the producers of the television program *ER* and requests from hospitals and doctors to buy the shirts by the dozens since they came out.
- The ACEP has used the T-shirts every spring since launch as a promotional item to attract new residents to the ER field.

Takeaway Tip

If you portray what you do as dry and boring, you won't draw in clients or new hires. Create a humorous or witty T-shirt to interject some fun and lighten up how you portray your business. T-shirts are a form of self-expression, and when people wear yours, they will feel infused with the light feeling you are trying to convey.

60. Thinking Outside the Box: Using College Lingo on an Unconventional Item to Attract Cult Status and Build Business on a College Campus

Creating branding that actually attracts college students is always a challenge: they're busy and don't care about advertising. Rather than reading billboards, they're tweeting and hanging out on Facebook. They're fast-forwarding through commercials. They are immune to your efforts. So when Hirons & Company was approached by B-Town Pizza, based in Bloomington, Indiana, to revamp its branding with a look that would resonate with Indiana University college students, Drew Hammond knew he had a challenge. "The primary goal was to create a brand that spoke directly to the college students," says Hammond of Hirons & Company. "We wanted the tone to be funny, interesting and authentic to their college experience."

Why It Works

Visually, the brand is designed to feel like stencil art. Simple shapes like the star and brackets create an abstract form representing the pizza box. The logo uses just two colors (crimson and black) and a simple brushing technique to get the intended look. "The hardest part was not over-thinking it," explained Hammond.

The pizza boxes, which are sure to litter more than a handful of college dorm rooms at Indiana University, is peppered with cheeky statements such as, "Your calculus book is the fourth leg of your sofa" that appeal to the college crowd. The statements also appear on T-shirts B-Town sells on its site.

Success Metrics

- The branding by Hirons & Company garnered three Gold ADDYs, the Gold Medal of advertising given by the American Advertising Federation.
- The design elements are used on pizza boxes, the website, T-shirts, and the restaurant's Facebook page, all with positive feedback.

Takeaway Tip

Talk the talk of your target audience. Use the words and phrases they use. Your message may not only resonate but achieve cult status. Oh, and put your messages on the things your target audience reads. If they don't read billboards, magazines, or newspapers, then put your message where they *do* read. It may be someplace unconventional (like a pizza box). But if it's one of the things they see and read, unconventional doesn't matter. And in the process, make your message look attractive in choice of fonts, colors, and other elements so that they can't *help* but read it.

61. An A Cappella Visual Promotion for Musicians: Attracting Your Target Market with a Banner Containing Images and No Words

The banner that rises above the newly converted warehouse in the Benton Harbor downtown arts district in Michigan has no words—it's strictly visual. Piano keys form the shape of a stairway at the top of the banner with a large quarter note at the bottom. The Quarternote Lofts are banking on the fact that its target clientele of music students and aficionados of the Citadel Dance and Music School—located on the first floor—will know what the symbol means.

Why It Works

There are four residential lofts (or living "quarters") above the Citadel Dance and Music School. Paula Bodnar Schmitt and writer Keith Oppenheim of the Bodnar Design Consultancy created the name and the symbols, which have become a beacon within the burgeoning arts district. Kenneth Ankli, owner, calls the banners, "a fitting exclamation point to the building's rehabilitation." He says the visual identity of the building has taken them from the ranks of "near tear-down" to a historical, avant garde mixed-use facility in a neighborhood that is now experiencing a renaissance.

Success Metrics

- Building owner Ankli says, "The sidewalks are busy, parking is scarce and the atmosphere is dynamic," due in part to the Quarternote Lofts identity and presence in this revitalized neighborhood.
- The building is 100 percent occupied. All four loft residences were immediately rented, and the Citadel Dance and Music School occupies the ground floor.

Takeaway Tip

A beautiful banner with images and no words can make a striking sign, and even serve as an outdoor work of art. A picture can be better than 1,000 words on a banner, especially if you're confident the market you are appealing to will recognize and find meaning in the images used in the banner.

62. Getting a Bright Start in Branding: Using Three-Dimensional Displays Integrated with a Sales Presentation

Sometimes a brochure just isn't enough to get your brand noticed. That's why Bright Starts, maker of baby toys, didn't just go outside of the box—it recreated the box—for its Brand Essence Toolbox. The Toolbox needed to effectively integrate the five brands that fall under Bright Starts. The pop-up board represents Bright Starts as the foundation, and the three stacking blocks are used to represent the technology, palettes, textiles, and characters of each brand. The Toolbox is used in retail presentations and to share with distributors. A presenter talks through each piece and stacks them, one on top of the other, and at the end of the presentation has demonstrated the building blocks of the brand.

Why It Works

"Our brand is very diverse and this tool was an interactive, dynamic way to bring the brand to life for an audience that needed to get a good baseline understanding of what our brand is about," says Lisa Connolly, director of brand management of Bright Starts.

The Toolbox is immediately engaging with its bright colors, diverse shapes, and attractive images. It immediately speaks to what the brand represents (baby products) with its simplistic shapes and toylike appearance.

The audience can interact with each block by pressing buttons that trigger giggling sounds or swinging the miniature cradle, which functions with the same technology as the actual product.

Success Metrics

- The Toolbox has been used in numerous vendor presentations with great feedback.
- Bright Starts successfully took five diverse brands and pulled them together to represent the whole.
- The Toolbox reinforced confidence in Bright Starts's brands and the brand strategy to its customers.

Takeaway Tip

Get away from traditional brochures if you want to make a splash with your presentation. A three-dimensional display that you assemble during your sales presentation is unexpected and therefore more memorable. And when the display represents your products, it better communicates the benefits of your offering.

63. Lunch Bags That Educate, Entertain, and Inspire: Maintaining a Strong Emotional Connection with Your Target Market Even as Your Brand Grows and Evolves

Kristi Thomas, the founder and CEO of Lunchology, started out with a simple goal. To help daughter Madison deal with separation anxiety at school, she started drawing pictures and inspirational messages on her daughter's brown paper lunch bags, adding "little love notes from home." They served their purpose, helping Madison get through that difficult time. Soon her daughter's classmates and their moms were asking for their own lunch bag designs . . . and a business was born.

Eight years later, the company offers more than 1,000 themed bags sets intended to "educate, entertain and inspire" kids. The bags are now carried by upscale grocery markets and gift retailers across the United States, including Whole Foods. Thomas no longer draws the designs herself. As she says, as the business grew, she had to start taking off hats. Besides, she acknowledges that if you want to grow you must bring in people who are more competent than you are at certain things. Graphic designer Kenny Kiernan breathed new life into her original designs and now creates all new designs.

Why It Works

Lunchology knows its target market well: both the moms who buy the bags and the kids who clamor for them. To strengthen the strong emotional connection that both moms and kids have with the product, the bags are intentionally designed to continue to look like a "Mom" hand drew the messages: no slick commercial images here. All messaging is positive, loving, and uplifting, meant to build self-esteem and pump up fragile young egos. Some messages are educational, containing small factoids. For example, one such factoid describes how the microwave oven was discovered. The drawings are friendly, too, and childlike. The company is introducing its first four-color lunch bag, but until now, all drawings have been in black (to simulate a pencil or pen drawing).

Success Metrics

- The lunch bags are now carried in 1,500 retail outlets across the United States.

- Lunchology just landed a three-year nationwide contract with a division of Staples.
- In a case of bad-news good-news, the lunch bags have become so popular that imitators have popped up, prompting Lunchology to enforce trademark rights more than once.

Takeaway Tip

Emotion underpins and informs our buying decisions. For some products, emotion is at the center. Make sure your brand continues to maintain that emotional connection and authenticity that attracted your target market in the first place. Small details in your designs—your choice of images, fonts, and colors—convey emotion. Even as you grow your business and your brand expands, choose outside design help that shares your vision and will extend it, not change it.

64. Making Friends Globally: Using Free Samples to Promote a Book and a Socially Responsible Business

Fair trade—meaning paying suppliers from poor countries fairly for their efforts—is a hot topic in these times of socially responsible businesses. Stacey Edgar's company, Global Girlfriend, is an example of a fair trade company. It is a multimillion dollar company that specializes in handmade, fairly traded, eco-conscious apparel and accessories made by women all over the world. To better tell the story behind Global Girlfriend and bring fair trade practices to life, Edgar wrote a book called *Global Girlfriends*. The word *Girlfriends* is plural in part because the book is about the women who supply the products the company sells. Some of these women, from Nepal, appear on the cover of the book.

To promote awareness of the book, Edgar created a book signing invitation postcard that depicts the book on one side, with details about the book signing on the other, and handed them out at professional events. Not unusual, right? But what makes the postcard stand out is that attached to it was one of the fair-trade coin purses sold by Global Girlfriend.

Why It Works

It has synergies on several levels. It's a product sample attached to a printed promotional piece so that people can identify the brand origin. But it also is about using a branded book to create crossover appeal and awareness for a brand. Says Edgar, "If you like our products (customer) I hope you might read the stories behind the products in the book.

If you like the book (reader) I hope you might be inspired to try some of the great products the women make."

As an actual product that people can use, it tends to be valued enough not to be thrown out like so many items given at events.

And as Edgar says, "When we give products it lets us re-order with our groups who make the goods so it's a win-win for our brand and the women behind the products."

Success Metrics

- Book sales have been excellent.
- As a business with a social conscience, it's not all about money. Says Edgar, "I hope telling the artisans' stories will help them to grow their businesses: first through growth in our orders to them due to increased business driven by new customers who read the book and second through other importers who may choose to work with them."

Takeaway Tip

A branded book that tells the story behind your business is excellent for growing awareness, among other things. Don't pass up an opportunity to promote your business with the book, which has crossover appeal. One way to do that is to offer a product sample to promote the book.

65. Much Ado about Nothing: A Campaign with Clever Props and Giveaways Transforms a Hard-to-Appreciate Concept into Something Real and Tangible

Many people think that there's nothing you can do to end hunger. The Rhode Island Community Food Bank challenged that perception with an aggressive campaign that sold empty cans of "nothing" for $2.99, raised awareness, and brought in record breaking donations. Unemployment is high, jobs continue to be scarce, and the outlook for the Rhode Island economy is still bleak. In this climate, eradicating hunger seems insurmountable.

- There was an increase of 16 percent in new e-mail addresses from donors and supporters.

Why It Works

By treating this campaign like a new product launch, NAIL Communications used the marketing muscle of branding to sell Nothing. The cans could be bought at more than 135 local stores. Retail partners were strategically selected where people were already thinking about food and feeding families. Online donations provide opportunities for people to become engaged as regular donors and supporters. Younger donors typically respond to tangible fund-raising objectives. Creating a real can that you could hold in your hand challenged the fact that hunger is often a silent problem. The cans represented 10 pounds of nutritious food—and there was a slit in the side of the can to serve as a "bank" and fund-raising tool as well.

Success Metrics

- More than 14,000 cans of Nothing were purchased, and $20,000 in donations were returned in the cans to the Rhode Island Community Food Bank.
- Online there were 49,816 home page views, 14,442 YouTube video views, and increased social networking with Facebook up 66 percent and Twitter followers up 47 percent.

Takeaway Tip

Does your organization tackle problems that are hard to understand or seemingly impossible to ever solve? Use clever props and giveaways to represent intangible concepts and transform them into something concrete and relevant. For example, to represent a concept like hunger that may seem alien to well-fed Americans, create a can of nothing. Suddenly a situation that few have experienced becomes real when you can see it and touch it.

Chapter 3

POWER TO THE PRINT ITEM!
POSTERS, BROCHURES, POSTCARDS, AND LOGOS STILL
PACK A PUNCH IN THE INTERNET AGE

Some say print is dead, and we thought this section might be a bit smaller than the others. . . . Yet to our surprise, we found that small businesses still consider print viable—and essential—even in the age of the Internet. Print can make a bigger impression and last longer than online e-mails that are as easy to delete as they are to deliver. Print and visual elements are a key component of a branding strategy for companies in a wide range of industries. Myers Constructs, a residential renovation company, built their marketing campaign around postcards of renovation images so beautiful that they become coveted objects people save until they are ready for their own projects. Posters still rule in Fort Point, where thousands turn out for an art festival. Even the online sensation, the TED conference, launches in India with a unique and powerful program . . . in print. Whether it's a business card (still the small-business person's best outreach tool) or a leave-behind card like the one used by Sickday, a contemporary medical service that makes house calls, print continues to be part of the smart marketer's arsenal of tools. The visual marketing projects highlighted in this chapter are distinctive, are attractive, and, most of all, fit the message of the company, service, or product they promote.

66. Who Is Keith Beith? Capitalizing on a Unique Name and Interjecting Friendliness to Differentiate a Business

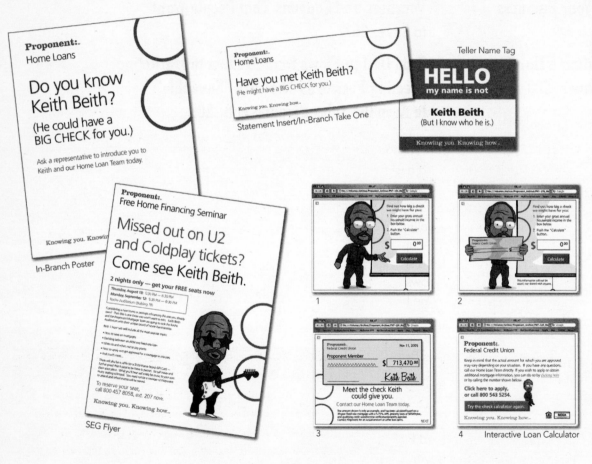

In-Branch Poster

Statement Insert/In-Branch Take One

Teller Name Tag

SEG Flyer

1

2

3

4   Interactive Loan Calculator

"How often do you get to play with a client name that rhymes?" asks Billy Joe Pyle, creative director of Mint Advertising in Philadelphia. Believe it or not, Keith Beith is not a character from a Dr. Seuss book. He's a real person and willing participant in a campaign that generated more than $14 million in a new mortgage loans for Proponent Federal Credit Union.

HELLO
my name is not

Keith Beith
(But I know who he is.)

Knowing you. Knowing how.℠

Who is
Keith Beith?
And why does he want
to give you a BIG check?

For rehirance, ask any representative.

Why It Works

Keith Beith, the senior loan officer at Proponent, is depicted as a cartoon character who guides you through the thicket of mortgage loan processing. The campaign provides an unusual comic approach to a traditional and serious topic. It's friendly and nonthreatening and invites customers to get to know the person who will help them save money on their mortgages. Tellers wore name badges that said, "Hello, my name is not Keith Beith. (But I know who he is.)" A variety of media featured a cartoon Keith Beith with a witty quip and a smile on newsletters, statement stuffers, direct mail, in-branch posters, and online calculators. Keith Beith grew up in Freehold, New Jersey, in a small town where everyone knows your name. Beith says his name has always been more of an asset than a liability. "Once it's heard, it's never forgotten," says Beith.

Success Metrics

- More than $14 million in new loans was generated by the promotion—well beyond projections.
- Return on investment in gross revenue/cost was 5,600 percent.
- The personal goodwill generated by promoting Keith Beith and his cartoon likeness supports Proponent's positioning as a friendly bank where your neighbors may be found.

Takeaway Tip

In some industries it can be hard to differentiate one company from another. Capitalize on a unique name to create a memorable character to demystify a process and interject friendliness and lighthearted humor into your marketing.

67. Face-to-Face Illustrations: Establishing an Identity That Allows Your Team Members to Express Themselves

Who are Gerald and Cullen Rapp, and why do they make their illustrators draw pictures of them in face-to-face profile? The personal touch is alive and well in the hands of this prestigious agency that represents the world's most respected and innovative conceptual artists. Gerald & Cullen Rapp is considered by many in the industry to be the premier source for editorial and advertising art. The visual gimmick that has become their brand has been done over and over again for many years and keeps looking fresh and unexpected. As the artwork gets more abstract, the concept becomes even more endearing. Could this be the concept that inspired the Absolut Vodka iconic campaign?

In 1944 Cullen Rapp formed an art studio in New York City, and he used a portrait of himself as the logo for his company. In 1974, when his son Gerald joined him, he added his name to the company and illustrator Gerry Gersten drew a new illustration showing the profiles of the two owners. For many years this was the logo for the agency. But a funny thing happened, and it began gradually and in an organic way.

Why It Works

Illustrators are creative people who are not used to doing the same thing over and over again, and they don't necessarily like to see another illustrator's drawing on their promotional page. So, some of the artists began to draw their own modified versions of the portraits and created their own logos to appear on their promotional pages. As more editorial artists joined the agency, there seemed to be more interest in transforming the logo into their own individual style. "The campaign was an ideal way to show off the creativity of our talent. It was immediately a big hit with art directors, designers and illustrators," says founder Jerry Rapp.

This brand continues to be fresh and innovative as new artists apply their own style and interpretation to the themes. The painter Georges Seurat once said, "Originality depends only on the character of the drawing and the vision peculiar to each artist." The ever-changing logo becomes a new piece of art in the hands of each artist.

Success Metrics

- Art directors and designers love the campaign, and the agency, which represented 25 artists in 1989, when the campaign began, now has more than 60 artists under contract.
- The campaign represents a strong brand that promotes the reputation of Gerald & Cullen Rapp and has attracted the high-caliber artists who have joined the agency. Creating a Rapp logo is a rite of passage among up-and-coming artists.

Takeaway Tip

Create a visual "theme" for how your associates, or employees, present themselves as part of the firm. Let them be creative—but within a defined framework. They will feel a part of the business, while also reinforcing the firm's signature brand identity. Having your team members present themselves creatively can even enhance the firm's brand, particularly if the firm is in certain creative fields where visual creativity is highly valued.

68. Business Cards Get Social: Creating Business Cards That Mimic Social Media Icons Opens New Market

We've come to associate a rounded square shape with social media icons. Custom printing service Jakprints recognized the power in this iconic shape. In 2010 it designed a special business card product called Favicards. Favicards are cards for people to share their social media profiles. They are 2-inch by 2-inch squares, with the recognizable rounded corners of social media icons—instead of the old school business card shape and size.

Jakprints created an interactive online app so that people can design their own Favicards online in minutes. Customers can choose a social media design mimicking an icon for Facebook, Twitter, YouTube, iTunes, or Flickr, or they can customize the cards with their own design. They can add data on the back with contact information, Web addresses, and QR codes.

Why It Works

This business card starts conversations and stands out because of its unusual shape. It signals that the user is in the know . . . and one of the social media cognoscenti. The cards appeal to musicians, photographers, entrepreneurs, and social media enthusiasts.

More and more, connecting with people through social media channels takes precedence over having their e-mails and phone numbers. If we just know how to find someone on Twitter or Facebook, we can continue to network with them, without needing to know the rest of their contact details.

Success Metrics

- In less than a year since the product launch, Jakprints sold 54,850 Favicards to hundreds of customers.
- Favicards have burst into mainstream events like the New England Metal Festival, South by Southwest (SXSW), and others, targeting the core audience of musicians and independent artists.

— On the Front — — On the Back —

Check out my glasses!

facebook.com/vincefrantz

Takeaway Tip

Update a traditional element of your business with social media designs. Facebook, Twitter, and other social media are hot right now, and leveraging their popularity can make your business stand out, be memorable, and seem fresh and up-to-date.

69. Changing Perceptions One School at a Time: Using a Marketing Pamphlet to Update an Organization's Image

We are **Catlin Gabel.**
We are an independent, coeducational day school for interested, engaged, and creative students from preschool to twelfth grade.

We are dedicated to the teaching philosophy of progressive education and offer a challenging, innovative, and diverse curriculum. We celebrate the partnership between family and school and strive to develop a community of great thinkers.

What do you do when the perception of your day school is pretentious and outdated? You refresh your image with some powerful marketing. That's just what Portland-based Catlin Gabel School did. The private school for preschoolers up to 12th graders realized that their community had unjustly created the opinion that it was stodgy, stuffy, and so-so at educating its students. In order to refute the rumors, Catlin Gabel hired a makelike design studio to create a fun and fresh pamphlet that expressed what the school is really about.

A makelike writer attended class with the students, and an illustrator mapped out the landscape by hand. Then, as makelike designer Mary Kysar explains, they created a three-color publication that may be read as a traditional eight-page brochure or unfolded and viewed as a large poster.

Why It Works

The pamphlet plays on the rumors about the school ("Catlin Gabel is not . . .") and highlights its progressive perspective. It provides a surprising amount of information on the school's teaching philosophy, as well as a childlike illustration that provides personalized insight into what the school is really like.

This pamphlet turns the traditional private school brochure on its ear by making it fun and engaging to read. "In the end, the piece is a true reflection of the innovative and infectious spirit of the school," says Kysar. "Learning about the school by mirroring the student experience allowed us to make a piece that spoke to them in their own voice."

Success Metrics

- The brochure became an effective tool for admissions to raise interest in potential students.

- The brochure went out as a mailer to key constituents, is hosted as a flipbook on the school's website, and became a poster tacked to classroom walls and students' bedrooms.
- Children and adults alike enjoy looking at the map and finding their corners of the campus and reading the words attached.

Takeaway Tip

Reputation isn't permanent. A solid marketing piece can help shift perception away from rumor and toward the truth.

70. Meeting Artists in Their Natural Habitat: Creating a Series of Posters Conveys the Range and Variety of a Large Event

Extra! Extra! Read all about it! Is the circus in town? What are those big, bold turn-of-the-century–style posters all about? The annual studio tour and art sale at the Fort Point Artist's Neighborhood was promoted with not one, but eight distinctive posters celebrating the art and the artists from the famed arts district in Boston. And although neither the fort nor the hill with a point still exists, the name Fort Point has endured as the home to artists for more than a quarter of a century. The posters feature work from performance art to jewelry, from photography to hand-sewn baby clothes. The series attracted a wide range of serious art buyers, collectors, and anyone who wanted to see new art or find a unique handcrafted gift.

There are many art shows in Boston during the fall, so designer Joanne Kaliontzis set out to distinguish 2010's annual show by emphasizing the opportunities to buy arts and crafts from a wide variety of real artists and craftspeople. At Fort Point you get to see the artists in their own studios, up close and personal, and Kaliontzis knew a single image was not

going to be enough to cut through the clutter. She said the posters needed to emphasize the character of the historic neighborhood and the accessibility of the artists while promoting the range of buying opportunities.

Why It Works

The posters were hung around the local neighborhood and in the Boston metro area, including large-format versions in the South Station and at the Prudential Mall. Digital images were distributed online via the website and were used by the artists for frequent Facebook postings. "This year's poster series was fresh and exciting," says Gabrielle Schaffner, FPAC executive director

and Open Studios coordinator. "They captured an essence of the neighborhood . . . and created a buzz of their own." The posters feature images of paintings and photographs of the old mills and loft spaces from Fort Point combined with artifacts like a diamond ring, a stylish old sofa, or a steaming kettle. You get to see the style of different artists in the artwork as well as see real items you may want to purchase. The overall design motif for the series contained a distinctive striped background with large faded "wooden" block typefaces.

Using a historic style with a dash of humor in a series of posters and online graphics provided a fresh

way to promote the Fort Point Arts Community Open Studios event.

Success Metrics

- More than 5,000 people visited the waterfront neighborhood to see original creations and purchase artwork.
- A total of 150 painters, sculptors, ceramicists, jewelers, performance artists, fashion designers, book artists, and photographers participated in the program.

Takeaway Tip

When publicizing a large and varied event, create not just one poster but a series of posters with different imagery to strengthen your message with multiple exposures and convey the range of what attendees can expect.

71. The Omaha Cow and Snowboarding: Using an Iconic Symbol Updated with Current Culture to Create an Au Courant Logo

What visual symbol best represents the silicon prairie of Omaha? Drew Davies, Oxide Design creative director and founder, says that after a lot of soul-searching the answer was clear. The cow was the perfect tongue-in-cheek symbol for the city. "Special bonus? Cows are kitschy and kinda funny looking," adds Davies. The cow indeed became the central image in a campaign to attract creatives, entrepreneurs, and innovators to a weekend conference in Omaha founded by Jeff Slobotski and Dusty Davidson and produced by the *Silicon Prairie* News.

"The challenge when branding the Big Omaha conference was to pay homage to the history of Omaha, while recognizing its place as a leader in the digital and electronic development," says Davies.

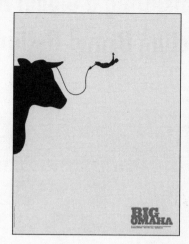

Why It Works

The identity needed to be uniquely "Omaha," while conveying the conference's core intent: bringing this key audience to the city. The creative team considered meatpacking, corn, plains, and even football. They spent a lot of time determining what things are uniquely specific to Omaha. With a rich heritage in the beef industry, the cow seemed best suited for the job.

The creative solution combines a shadow image of a very prominent cow (it is "BIG OMAHA" after all) with unexpected extreme sports images like snowboarding, bungee jumping, and car racing. The campaign was featured in posters displayed in coffee shops and businesses throughout the city of Omaha and online. The coordinated campaign included Twitter and a dedicated website that fueled word-of-mouth.

Davies says, "The brand itself plays on the whimsicalness of the event, and that carries through down to the tiniest pieces of the experience. From the moment our guests walk through the door, we want them to live and breathe Big Omaha, to interact with the space, and to engage with those around them."

Success Metrics

- In only its second year, the conference doubled its attendees to more than 500.
- Of the attendees, 60 percent came from Nebraska; the balance came from 22 different states.

- The Big Omaha posters received design awards from the Nebraska chapter of the AIGA and *Communications Arts* magazine.

Takeaway Tip

When creating a logo, embrace a symbol that is already well known but render it with an updated, fresh approach. By emphasizing heritage while appealing to current culture, you convey the best of both worlds.

72. Translating a Global Brand into Local Currency: Making an Existing Brand Design Resonate in a Different Country

When TED, the nonprofit devoted to "Ideas Worth Spreading," decided to host its first conference in India, the company knew it had to translate its well-known brand into one that both citizens of India and the international visitors to the conference would relate to. TED retained the design services of Albertson Design to take on the mission. The result? A 200+-page book that is functional but retains fun design elements that encourage attendees to keep it as a memento.

David Albertson of Albertson Design said he wanted to "leverage the existing TED brand, with an Indian twist."

Why It Works

Thicker than most conference guides, TEDIndia's book features an open spine, making note taking easier; a cover that converts to a poster for added keepsake potential; and "secret" edge-trim messaging guaranteed to make owners of the book smile with delight.

The cover features slices of photographs and digitized photos of Indians. Since people like seeing images of others who look like them, TED succeeds in translating its brand locally in India. The book is filled with color photographs and bright images, guaranteeing the eye will never have a dull moment. And while many may not hang their TEDIndia poster up on their wall, the engineering of the poster-turned-book-cover is sheer genius.

Success Metrics

- TEDIndia's first and only event had sold-out audiences of 1,000 attendees from 46 countries.
- The event successfully brought the TED brand to South Asia.
- The book is considered by TED to be one of its most successful guides so far.

Takeaway Tip

Branding doesn't always translate globally. What was once a concern of large companies only is now a matter for small businesses to consider as more and more operate as "micro-multinationals." By taking a fresh look from a different country's perspective, a brand can adapt its existing design with local elements that are inclusive and effective.

73. Getting to the Point in Acupuncture: Combining Professional Design with Do-It-Yourself Execution Keeps Expenses in Line

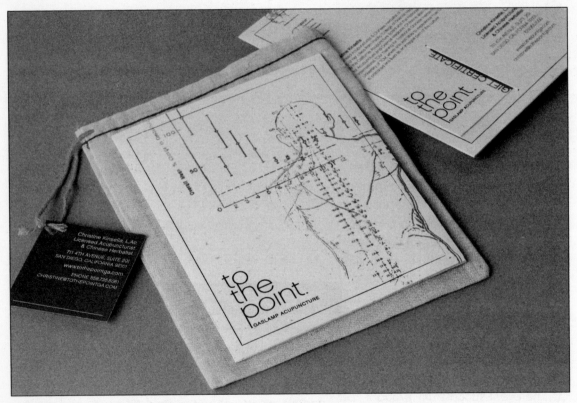

Good design and printing don't have to require a business loan. Just ask To The Point Acupuncture. When the company launched its acupuncture business in San Diego, it needed a clever brochure that would bring in new clients. The design budget was small, but To The Point retained Bex Brands to create a design that the company could modify over time. And because the start-up had limited funds, it wanted a brochure it could reproduce in smaller quantities without paying too much.

Why It Works

Some business owners don't think of design as being flexible or even affordable. Yet Bex Brands worked with To The Point to create a versatile business card and brochure.

"We were able to create fun, professional and eye-catching brochures by investing a small amount of money on good paper, then creating a template that my client could edit as her company grew, and simply have it copied at a local copy shop. We were able to add color at a low expense by developing a set of oversized rubber stamps," says Becky Nelson of Bex Brands.

Bex Brands provided a sort of map for the design so To the Point would know where to place the stamps, which allowed the company to print and put together brochures as needed at a low cost.

Success Metrics

- Within its first year of business, To the Point added staff to accommodate its burgeoning business.

- The owner of To the Point has become a well-respected businessperson in her field and is involved with the Gaslamp Quarter Business Association.
- To the Point consistently appears on many "Best of . . ." lists in San Diego for acupuncture.

Takeaway Tip

Good design doesn't have to be expensive, and a hybrid of quality work and do-it-yourself does exist. By creating professionally designed components that can be updated and swapped out by the client as needs change, a marketing brochure can stay relevant. And your investment in design can reap returns for years.

74. An Image Consultant Makes a Great First Impression: Differentiating a Personal Brand by Conveying Your Personality

Gretchen Ditto helps clients craft the perfect first impression. By selecting the right clothes and discovering what colors complement a client's natural coloring, she establishes a distinctive style for each client. Ditto knows that the right professional image can bring out a positive attitude and become a powerful tool in advancing a career. Ditto did a lot of online research before she launched her business. As an image consultant, she's very aware of how her brand should look. Ditto stresses that she must have a great brand because her business is all about image. But how does an image consultant create the right image for herself? She turned to professional designer Katrina Hase at the Mix Creative in Minneapolis to build a personal, professional brand.

Why It Works

Hase created a simple Art Deco typographic logo for Ditto & Co. that aligns with the tagline, "Transforming Style." The website quotes Yves St. Laurent, who said, "Fashions fade. Style is eternal." It's not about fads, and it's much more than just a new hairdo and makeup. The visual marketing of Ditto & Co. is whimsical and friendly, yet may be taken seriously. Hase designed four illustrated note cards with hand-drawn illustrations that are manipulated by computer with a motif that reproduces the Ditto brand typeface. Ditto uses the note cards as lead generators, leave-behinds, and follow-up reminders. The cards have a personalized, greeting card feel. "We wanted the look and feel to be more casual and social while still clearly branded as Ditto & Co.," says Hase. The illustrated motif continues on stationery, website, and classically designed gift certificates.

Success Metrics

- Ditto reports that clients and prospects often perceive Ditto & Co. as a franchise based on the professional branding.
- Ditto is a featured author in *Get Organized Today* (Power Dynamics Publishing). She attributes the design of her website and brand as the reason she was interviewed by the *Minneapolis Star Tribune* as an expert in career style.
- Since launching the Ditto & Co. identity and website, Ditto has built a steady schedule of paid speaking engagements. The brand has given her enough credibility that she no longer has to speak at free events.

Takeaway Tip

Done right, your professional image will advance your career and position you to achieve goals that once seemed out of reach. Capture your personality and style in your marketing collaterals to differentiate your personal brand.

75. A Recipe for Success in Publishing: Using Beautiful, Evocative Images Reinforces the Essence of a Publication

Why is there a big red ripe tomato on the cover of the cookbook *The Gourmet Bachelor?* Chad Carns, art director, writer, and aspiring celebrity chef, chose the image because it visually expresses what the book is all about: using easy-to-find fresh ingredients to cook impressive meals. People told him to put a photo of himself cooking on the cover. "But I'm not the bachelor—I'm the guy who knows how to help bachelors cook. The readers are the bachelors," says Carns with a grin. (He is actually married.) First and foremost, he wanted the cover to feature delicious food and to be universal.

Why It Works

Carns is the modern entrepreneurial Renaissance man—part publisher, writer, art director, marketer, and spokesperson. He spent the good part of a year travelling the country promoting his book. Carns believes his book could not have been produced in any other era. The convergence of low-cost digital publishing and social media, combined with a tough economy, allowed him to collaborate with top-notch creatives to produce a high-concept, professional book. "At least 30 people helped me put this book together," says Carns.

Carns spent three years creating, publishing, and launching his book. He initially sold it exclusively on his own website and then worked out distribution deals with Amazon and Barnes & Noble. Will he devote himself to being the "bachelor gourmet" chef for the rest of his life? That's his short-term goal. For the long term, he strives to become the preeminent food and wine communications guru.

Success Metrics

- National media exposure has been phenomenal. A Google search will generate more than 100 listings of *Gourmet Bachelor* media postings.
- Carns cooked a three-course gourmet dinner live on the Miami edition of the *Today* show, and it was broadcast throughout Florida, Central America, and South America.
- *Marie Claire* published Carns's Thanksgiving dinner menu for bachelorettes.

Takeaway Tip

When publishing a book, e-book, or any publication, choose images for the cover and inside the book that evoke an experience of the senses, and by their nature convey to readers, in a variety of subtle ways, what the book is about. Taking the time to find that one great image will pay off.

76. The Art of Making House Calls: Using Simple Logo Imagery That Marries Traditional Values with a Modern Business

Looks like you have to go to the big city to find someone willing to make old-fashioned medical house calls. A service called Sickday provides prompt medical attention in the comfort of your home, office, or hotel in New York City.

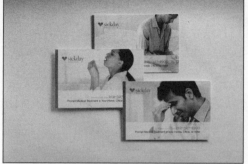

Why It Works

The Sickday brand, created by YYES, a Los Angeles design studio, is based on an image of a heart made from a folded Band-Aid. This strikes a nice balance between professionalism of health care and a feeling of compassion. Sickday founder Naomi Friedman says that YYES delivered the perfect sentiment for their brand and incorporated not only what they needed at launch, but every element they foresaw in their future. "They listened to us the way we listen to patients," Friedman says.

Since follow-through is so critical in successful medical care,

Sickday checks back with each patient after every visit. Get Well cards were designed so that the Sickday physician associates may leave notes and instructions. "We use the Get Well cards daily and we provide the cell phone number of practitioners to create ongoing access and availability during the course of illness," adds Friedman.

Success Metrics

- Market awareness of Sickday has increased as physicians across the country express interest in franchising the concept. Friedman says her immediate plans are to expand into the five boroughs of New York City.

- Patients hear about Sickday primarily through word of mouth or by searching for care on the Internet. Those who find them online often attribute their call to the look and feel of the branding and patient testimonials.
- Sickday serves thousands of New Yorkers and thousands of visitors to New York each year.

Takeaway Tip

Use simple imagery to bring traditional values (such as caring) into the logo and identity of a thoroughly modern business. When traditional values are at the heart of the service that your clients want, even if it's a 21st century business model, it's important that both the traditional and the modern be represented.

77. An Unorthodox Community Campaign Promotes Kindness: Using a Powerful Name to Drive Action

Deanna Harms of the Greteman Group, a design firm in Kansas, says that she launched Do the Deed to celebrate and inspire simple acts of kindness, one deed at a time. Do the Deed has inspired thousands of nice tweets and physical acts of kindness through Kansas and beyond. Several schools and churches have used Do the Deed as class projects, and Girl Scouts have distributed deed cards. The *Wichita Eagle* and *Fast Company* challenged readers to pass on the cheer. Many generous partners ran ads and billboards or posted yard signs and sidewalk stencils. A class at Wichita State University has taken on Do the Deed as a semester-long project.

The Do the Deed kit includes a program sheet with logos, stencils, posters, and outreach guidelines. Videos and photos may be viewed and shared online, and you may even track your progress in doing good deeds. It can be as simple as smiling at a stranger. Some of the most popular deeds are:

- Grabbing a shopping cart in the parking lot and taking it into the store with you
- Leaving the waiter a little extra
- Writing to a former schoolteacher

Why It Works

Humor plays a significant role in distinguishing the campaign. The blunt name—Do the Deed—stops people in their tracks. The logo features bright colors and bold type with an abstract dove ascending on the right. It's confident and playful at the same time and would look great on a bumper sticker. The campaign benefits from many applications from billboards to small buttons, and the viral nature of the videos and tweets allows it to spread easily through social media. All promotional materials drive people to the website, which offers deed suggestions and a place to log in and track your own deeds.

Success Metrics

- Within the first month, the *Wichita Eagle* ran online ads that garnered almost 450,000 impressions and 1,000 clicks.
- The Do the Deed video received almost 11,000 views, and 3,200 people visited the website.
- Miss Kansas, Lauren Werhan, adopted Do the Deed as her platform in the Miss America Pageant. She spoke about the initiative throughout Kansas and to the nation in Las Vegas at the national competition in 2011.

Takeaway Tip

Attach a memorable name (using alliteration, rhythmic cadence, and a built-in call to action by the choice of words) to a marketing campaign to serve as a strong call to action.

78. A Communications Firm Stands Out: Using Unconventional Visuals Instead of Cookie-Cutter B2B Design Gets Attention

For business services, standing out in a sea of competition can often be a challenge. It certainly was for the interMediator group. This full-service consultancy, focused on media and communications, wanted to get away from its cookie-cutter website and design elements. The firm retained John Pirman to update the logo and create graphics to illustrate the business concepts of the company: strategic planning, turnaround management, recruitment and development, sales management, and strategic communications.

"Most of my clients have their roots in print media, and particularly newspapers," says Henry Scott of the interMediator group. "The logo is intended, with its typeface, to reference

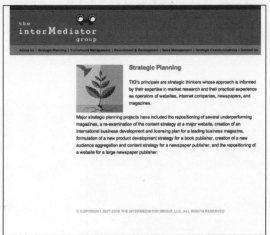

the old-fashioned world of type while also, through the name and unusual use of upper- and lowercase letters to suggest a new approach."

Why It Works

This is an industry where visual appeal is often forgotten. By pulling together the illustrated business concepts on the website, as well as on stationery, business cards, and marketing collateral, the interMediator group succeeds in being noticed.

"I believe really cool design sends a powerful message, one that isn't easily expressed in words. John Pirman's work signaled that my firm is at the top of its game professionally, but also that it is unconventional. Those are both aspects of my work that I try hard to promote," explains Scott.

Success Metrics

- While reactions to the previous design were lukewarm at best, the new design is getting applause from clients and media types.

- Having a cohesive design element across all collateral helps the firm prove that it is not a "kitchen table operation."
- The firm now has a clear modern visual solution that reflects its attitude and style.

Takeaway Tip

B2B marketing doesn't have to be boring, and, in fact, it shouldn't be. Create a consistent design theme across various collateral pieces, using unconventional and unexpected visual elements, to make a business services firm in a traditional market stand out and be remembered.

79. Is Your Name Defining You . . . Negatively? Renaming a Business Leads to More Sales

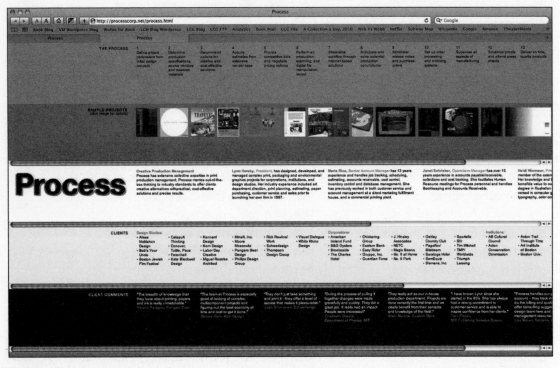

Upon hearing the name Clements Horsky Creative Directions, you probably have no clue what the company does. The print production management firm realized this problem and went to Visual Dialogue and Rick Rawlins Work to get help rebranding both its name and its marketing material. Despite the fact that the company handles print production for designers, its own marketing collateral had an "amateurish and haphazard look," according to Fritz Klaetke of Visual Dialogue.

PROCESS CORP Creative Production Management
MAIL 816 Depot Road Boxborough, MA 01719
TEL 617-650-0191
EMAIL lynn@processcorp.net

Playing on the four-color process inks common in printing as well as the process of design and print production, Visual Dialogue helped rebrand the company with a new name, "Process," and updated the company's logo, business papers, ads, and website.

Why It Works

If you're a designer (Process's target audience), you get it. The play on the name is a sort of inside joke, and the graphics across all channels exemplify this play. In no way will this design be a wallflower in its industry: It demands attention.

"The Process rebranding acted as a catalyst to increase our professional presence to our established client base and develop new opportunities," says Lynn Horsky, president of Process.

Success Metrics

- Process increased its profile among the design community in greater Boston, becoming the go-to print production managers for leading design firms.
- For the two years after upgrading its brand identity and website, Process's client base increased by 5 percent.

- The website also helped spur referrals, and several large projects were directly initiated by client visits to the site.

Takeaway Tip

Sometimes everything's in a name, and it can stand in your way to success. Survey people to find out if your brand's name speaks to what you want it to stand for; if not, do some rebranding to get on track.

80. A Condo Development Has Historical Charm: Incorporating Heritage into Marketing Visuals to Emphasize an Offering's Key Selling Points

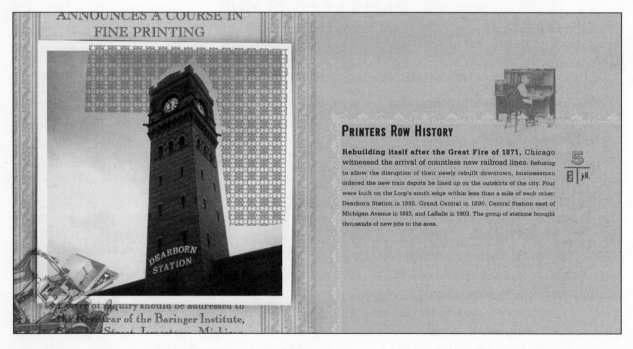

Printers Square, one of the largest residential conversions in Chicago, is named for the legendary industry of the 1900s. When this 350-unit development converted from apartments to condos, a marketing kit created by Firebelly Design was created to appeal to first-time buyers and young professional seeking a touch of luxury at a reasonable price.

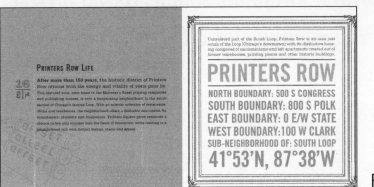

PRINTERS SQUARE

Why It Works

"What made this so successful," says Dawn Hancock, creative director at Firebelly Design, "was that the client was hands off and let us do what we do best." The JDL Development firm was more familiar selling higher-end properties. "We knew the neighborhood and the history of printing and that worked to our advantage," says Hancock. The design features classic-type styles and embellished illustrations that evoke the early 1900s and combines this with current photography, making them current and culturally relevant for modern lifestyles. Firebelly created targeted sales brochures for prospective buyers dedicated to studios, one-bedroom, and two-bedroom units. Then they designed a neighborhood guide that could

be used in combination with any of the sales brochures. The design team traced the floor plans from the 1970s and purposefully kept a hand-drawn style that captured the charm of the properties. The neighborhood guide became the most important tool in the marketing plan. People kept them and even displayed them as coffee table books.

Success Metrics

- The 350-unit development completely sold out, with 80 percent being sold within six weeks.
- A total of 400 people signed up online for a VIP list that was

promoted with marketing materials and text messaging.
- The program won numerous design awards, including Newberry Library's John M. Wing Foundation on the History of Printing collection, Chicago Design Archive, American Graphic Design Awards, and *Best of Brochure Design* 9.

Takeaway Tip

When history and heritage play a role in your offering, make sure you capture that to emphasize your key selling points. Images and design can uniquely capture that sales advantage in a way that words alone cannot.

81. HR with a Personal Touch: Using a Descriptive Name and a Caricature for a Consulting Business Sets You Apart

When you think of human resources (HR), you may think of complicated procedures for managing employees or programs with hard-to-remember acronyms and overwhelming bureaucracy. Wouldn't it be nice if someone could hold your hand, figuratively, and guide you through the thicket of regulations and recommended guidelines? That's where The HR Lady comes in.

Why It Works

Denise G. Scholl-Serrett is a certified benefits professional with the HR designations and accreditations associated with leading HR professionals. She wanted to distinguish her services from a crowded field of consultants. PowerBand Graphics created a brand around Denise's personality that is unique and funny. "If a business card can express 'energy' then mine certainly does," says Scholl-Serrett. The HR Lady brand is an easy conversation starter that has made networking easier. The imagery has a lot of gusto, yet it can still be taken seriously. After all, when you want to know how to protect your business against sexual harassment claims, you have to go to a trusted source. The bold caricature of the owner has a striking resemblance to Scholl-Serrett, who provides professional services with a personal touch.

Success Metrics

- The HR Lady saw sales double in the last two quarters of the first year in business.
- The branding opened doors at a well-established college with a continuing education department offering classes to business professionals. Each class appearance introduces Scholl-Serrett to 15 new prospects.
- As a new consultant, Scholl-Serrett is establishing reciprocal relationships with business associates where the brand brings a focused message and credibility.

Takeaway Tip

Why spend a lot of time explaining your business services or trying to differentiate yourself from dozens of other consultants when your name and business card can do it for you? Choose a descriptive straightforward moniker for your business and add a smidgen of personality in the form of a caricature of the owner. Together they will define your business and make it memorable.

82. All That Jazz, Funk, Blues, Pop, and Hip-Hop: Making Modifications in Your Imagery Can Appeal to a Younger Audience

The SaskTel Saskatchewan Jazz Festival is a venerable music festival that needed to broaden its approach and attract younger audiences. Each summer, more than 70,000 music fans head to the city of Saskatoon in Canada to enjoy a program of diverse music genres. A new marketing effort was created to attract the 18- to 35-year-old demographic.

The SaskTel Saskatchewan Jazz Festival had been expanding its lineup to include groups that appeal to younger audiences, and now it needed to freshen up its visual marketing to communicate this to new audiences. Rob Maguire says that managing a festival is a lot like running a small business. He has a staff of three workers doing the administration, marketing, HR, and programming while he coordinates a large part-time and volunteer army to run the 10-day festival.

Why It Works

They turned to Dawn Hancock at Firebelly Design who created an "exploding speaker" as the central image to rebrand the festival. Hancock was tasked with making the imagery younger and edgier without alienating core jazz fans. The artwork looks more freeform and lively like hip-hop, yet it resonates like a jazz quartet kicking into gear with a new groove. By increasing the type size of "Festival" in the name and downplaying "Jazz," SaskTel Saskatchewan Jazz Festival ties itself to other younger and genre-jumping festivals like Lollapalooza, Coachella, and Bonnaroo.

Success Metrics

- Ticket sales for SaskTel Saskatchewan Jazz Festival increased by more than 30 percent with the new promotion.
- There were 70,000 attendees at more than 140 shows, and the 18- to 35-year-old demographic is growing.

Takeaway Tip

Not attracting younger audiences as your offering matures? Try branding modifications in the form of font sizes, bright colors, and imagery. The size of the words on a collateral are important in signaling the intention of your message to key audiences. And different images can make your offering appear up-to-date (versus stodgy) to appeal to younger demographics.

83. Communicate Issues Boldly: Using Bold Graphics to Drive Home the Importance of Messages

How does a small staff communicate a year's worth of work in one report? The Canadian HIV/AIDS Legal Network knows that the substance of their work is often highly technical. As a human rights organization, their advocacy work must be clearly communicated to funders, beneficiaries, and the public at large.

Why It Works

The designers at Soapbox, Inc., created a visual language for the critical initiatives and issues in ways that are accessible and compelling. The issues that the Canadian HIV/AIDS Legal Network tackle are highlighted with original artwork in bright and engaging colors.

For three years running, the annual reports have used a similar format of bold graphics alternating with an in-depth narrative punctuated with large numbers that scream out critical statistics and bring attention to the data that drive the organization as it fights the HIV/AIDS epidemic. Reports like *Deadly Disregard* include sound bites accompanied by powerful editorial illustrations that make the case for a needle exchange program. Readers of the reports are surprised to find such a wealth of statistical information and analysis in bite-sized installments with compelling graphics that make the abstract case for advocacy more relevant.

Success Metrics

- The Canadian HIV/AIDS Legal Network annual reports have won honors and awards from *Communication Arts*, International ARC Awards, the Advertising & Design Club of Canada (ADCC), and Design Edge Canada Regional Design Awards.
- The annual is published in *The Best of Brochure Design 11* from Rockport Publishers.

Takeaway Tip

When advocacy or social responsibility is part of your company's mission, visuals can define the mission in ways that words cannot. Use the power of artwork and design to convey sound bites that educate, persuade, and promote action. When people understand the issues, they are better prepared to act on them.

84. Eat or Be Eaten: Appealing to Local Tastes and Cultural Understanding in a Local Marketing Campaign

WHAT'S IN YOUR FUTURE?

EAT OR BE EATEN

SKUBA DESIGN STUDIO

When you work with clients across the country, sometimes the hardest challenge is marketing to your local audience. When Trace Newman Hayes decided to turn the focus of her New Orleans–based Skuba Design Studio locally, she had to look only at the "critters" found in southern Louisiana for inspiration.

"More than any place I have ever been, New Orleans has an abundance of critters that we have to live with," says Hayes, principal of Skuba. "I chose to use some of the critters to get our message out in a comical sort of way." Because New Orleans is "old school," says Hayes, she decided to go with a direct-mail postcard to reach potential new clients.

Why It Works

If you're local to New Orleans, you know the place nutria rats, crawfish, cicadas, oysters, and termites have in your world. Imagine getting a postcard with one of these undesirables in your mailbox. Attention getting? We think so. A series of six postcards were designed, each with its own locally grown creature. By coming up with witty taglines to accompany high-quality photos, Skuba's direct mail is hitting home with New Orleans businesses. Many want to keep the postcard as a work of art!

Success Metrics

- Within days of the initial postcard mailing, Skuba landed a new customer who had received a card.
- Skuba is redesigning a website for the top restaurant in the city whose chef competed on Bravo's *Master Chef* series.
- With only $250 spent on the direct-mail campaign, Skuba has already seen $6,000 to $7,000 in new revenue as a result of the campaign.

Takeaway Tip

Know your audience and what they have an emotional attachment to. When marketing to a local audience, incorporate local cultural icons and shared local experiences into your marketing materials. Although it might fall flat in another locale, that doesn't matter for a local campaign. You need appeal to only what your local audience will identify with.

85. Clothing for the Cosmopolitan Outdoorsy Type: Expressing the Importance of Form *and* Function for a Brand in Print

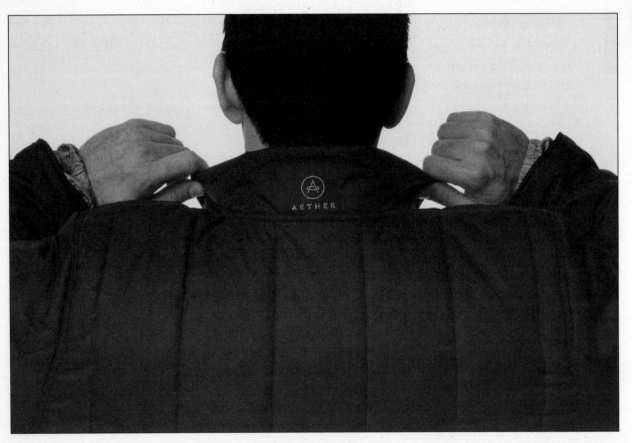

When you're hiking in the wilderness, you need clothing that protects you and keeps up with the latest high-action, fast-paced lifestyle of today's outdoor sportsmen and sportswomen. But there's no reason your clothing has to look frowsy. Aether Apparel provides urban-style fashion for outdoor enthusiasts.

Why It Works

The brand's sleek black and white logo design evokes "the heavens" with circles surrounding the "A" like clouds around a mountain peak. Aether, rooted in Greek mythology, means "upper air." The brand targets 30- to 40-year-olds rather than the snowboarding college students. The design by Carbone Smolan Agency is sophisticated with an aura of exclusivity. The design supports Aether sportswear for the outdoor enthusiast who wants function like PrimaLoft insulation and wind- and water-resistant materials without sacrificing modern design and aesthetics. Palmer West and Jonah Smith, founders of Aether Apparel, say that the design and function of their clothing should be equal. Lifestyle and environmental landscape photography was selected to support the brand's mission.

Success Metrics

- Aether's initial spike in growth continues to expand 20 to 25 percent each year.
- Aether has been prominently featured in GQ and the trend-spotting Cool Hunting website.
- J. Crew men's stores display Aether's line alongside iconic brands like Ray-Ban and Timex.

Takeaway Tip

When your product is about functioning well and looking good, use a simple, stylish logo design. Add a library of photographic images that express the experience that customers have when using your products. Together they will convey both form and function as being important.

86. Capturing the Legacy: Creating a Commemorative Book with High-Quality Graphics Conveys an Organization's Values

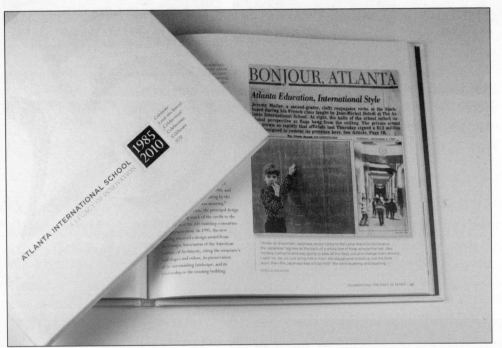

Educating children to be the next generation of global citizens is no easy feat, and doing so for 25 years is worth celebrating. That's why the Georgia-based Atlanta International School decided to retain the services of education marketing firm EM2 Design to assist in developing a commemorative book as part of the school's silver jubilee. The result is an attractive spiral-bound catalog/book that celebrates and highlights the Atlanta International School's legacy, events, milestones, and achievements. EM2's goal was to use photographs to illustrate the world from a different perspective, which fit in with the K-12 school's belief system.

Why It Works

Most private schools create a brochure or catalog, but it usually contains the same old information in mundane packaging. This commemorative book, however, evokes nostalgia with its spiral binding, reminiscent of school notebooks, but with a sophisticated twist. The photography and wording help the reader not only visualize the school's services but also understand the values the school brings to each of its students.

The book's use of die cut allows readers to peek at a smaller version of the image on the next page, and serves as a great three-dimensional visual element. Words in other languages are peppered throughout the copy, further enhancing that different global perspective that was the aim in the book's creation.

Success Metrics

- The book, which was sent to parents, faculty, alumni, and prospective students, has been met with resounding enthusiasm.
- The school, founded in 1984, has received accreditation from several international education institutions of excellence.

Takeaway Tip

Investing in a well-designed, visually stimulating commemorative book can help stakeholders connect with your organization's values and create a shared bond.

87. All for One and One for All: Repurposing Marketing Collateral on a *Very* Low Budget

Martín Perna DJs one night at Malverde, an Austin, Texas, nightclub, while Adrian Quesada spins another . . . and some nights they both perform. FÖDA Studio was given a budget for one poster but found out they needed to promote three events. So with a poster and a fat marker, Jett Butler designed one solution for three nights of entertainment.

Why It Works

Malverde is known for its hand-crafted specialty cocktails, extensive selection of tequila, local beers, and the soundtrack of Austin's best DJs. Owner Jesse Herman says that he really likes the design solution because it's a clever way to show how these two DJs collaborate. Sometimes you get both DJs; sometimes you get one. By combining them on one poster, it solidifies the relationship and establishes a consistency for the Wednesday night gigs. Butler's design uses a computer drawing technique that looks hand-drawn so that the marker "cross-outs" don't look all that out of place. Part of the appeal of this poster is the simplicity in its typographic design and layout.

Success Metrics

- Attendance at the club is usually standing room only, with about 150 people.
- In addition to paying for only one design, the ability to reuse the poster series for as long as the team of DJs is performing makes this solution very cost-effective.

Takeaway Tip

When you have a very small budget and can afford only one design piece but have to use it in different ways to promote different events, products, or services, you'd better put on your creative cap. Using a marker to cross out a name on a poster may not always be a good solution, but consider that a metaphor for finding low-cost ways to repurpose a single design to fit multiple situations, perhaps by dropping in different names or images using a computer graphics program. Necessity truly is the mother of invention.

88. Evoking Mood Through Design: Using Custom Invitations to Make Your Business Entertainment Last Beyond the Event

A masquerade ball is a special event, one filled with magic and mystery. So when Atlanta-based Sweet Life Events event planning company arranged the New Year's Eve Masquerade for the Benedicts of Atlanta, the company wanted a regal and luxurious invitation that reflected the mood of the evening. Jill Lynn Design stepped in to create a custom die-cut invitation on heavy black stock in the shape of a masquerade mask. Metallic gold ink and black ribbon added glamour and sophistication to the design.

Why It Works

Invitations are typically square, and not that original. Once you attend the event, you likely throw the invitation away, never to think about it or its sender again. But with the Masquerade Mask Invitation, it's a work of art in and of itself. The design serves as a souvenir of a special evening, and attendees of the New Year's Eve Masquerade kept their invitations as a memento of a thrilling event.

Because these aren't one-size-fits-all invitations, their complexity adds to their appeal. The layers of heavy paper and ribbon make it eye appealing from the moment one opens the envelope. The mask shape of the invitation fits in perfectly with the theme of the masquerade.

Success Metrics

- A total of 400 mask invitations were sent out to the Benedicts of Atlanta Social Club's members and guests for the New Year's Eve event.
- Due to the popularity of the invitation, Jill Lynn Design gets requests several times a month for the mask design.

Takeaway Tip

When your budget allows, go custom for design. Although an out-of-the-box invitation card will do the job for business entertainment, a custom-designed card reflecting the mood of your event will show your guests that you care about them enough to invest in a work of art. They'll remember you for it, which is especially important for businesses holding events as business entertainment.

89. High-End Rewards: Offering Upscale Coupons Grows Loyalty, Prevents Cancellations, and Sells Add-Ons

Groucho Marx never wanted to be a member of a club that would have him as a member. There are lots of reasons to avoid joining a club, so Manchester Athletic Club in Cambridge, Massachusetts, set out to attract new members and keep them with a welcome packet of coupons worth $270 in services.

Why It Works

The MAC Rewards Program provides a packet of coupons delivered in a handsome cardboard carrying case designed by Brian Conway. These are not your mother's supermarket coupons. They look more like award certificates, complete with ornate border designs in an upscale carrying case that brings a certain level of caché. The case encourages you to hang onto the coupons and use them over a period of months, instead of tossing them aside. Jay Herson, MAC's marketing director, says the investment in design has paid off by highlighting the value of the offers. These are high-end offers, not cheap discounts or leftovers. The research shows that the more members participate, the more invested they become in the club. The coupon packet increases membership loyalty and reduces cancellations.

Success Metrics

- Record numbers of new memberships were sold while the promotion ran, and overall membership revenues have increased by $100,000 for the two years the program has been running.
- The program increases participation in ancillary club services such as personal training and massages while increasing membership retention rates.

Takeaway Tip

Discounts don't need to look cheap. Package your coupons in an upscale manner to look like truly special offers. This increases the importance and perceived value of your offer. It builds loyalty and demand for upsales and cross-sales.

90. It's a Family Affair: Making Your Business Story Come to Life with a Beautifully Designed Print Piece

Una Collezione di Sapori

a selection of recipes from Ristorante Panorama

When Philadelphia's Penn's View Hotel celebrated its 20th anniversary, it wanted to offer a unique takeaway for guests of the festivities celebrating the family-owned and -operated hotel and its restaurant, Ristorante Panorama. Nicola Black Design suggested creating a booklet of family recipes to incorporate the restaurant's history into something personal and reflective of the family, who has made the business successful over the years. The booklet of recipes was a hit with party guests, so the hotel/restaurant decided to continue distribution beyond the event.

Why It Works

This hotel and restaurant have a story, and it's one that is told through good food. By providing a cookbooklet to guests, Penn's View successfully brings those guests into its collective family. It's clear that this isn't a corporate-run hotel, and its family history is one that makes the hotel that much more endearing.

"The family history element was important in creating the piece, so the recipes they've used throughout the 20 years of business seemed like a fun way to celebrate, literally giving clients a taste of their history," says designer Nicola Black. The booklet is filled with beautiful photography that encourages readers to attempt the recipes—and if they don't succeed, just visit Ristorante Panorama for the real deal.

Success Metrics

- In addition to being given as a gift at the anniversary event, the cookbooklet was also distributed at trade shows and to prospective hotel and restaurant guests, tourists, and supporters of the hotel/restaurant.
- The booklet was so successful that the hotel is discussing the creation of a full-size cookbook to sell.

Takeaway Tip

Sometimes you're too close to a story to see it, but step back and look at your business's history. You may find valuable marketing gold. Make your story come to life with a beautifully designed print item that tells the story in a way that customers will want to keep it.

91. An Industrial Business Bucks the Trend: Expressing Quality Through Color and Design Becomes a Competitive Advantage

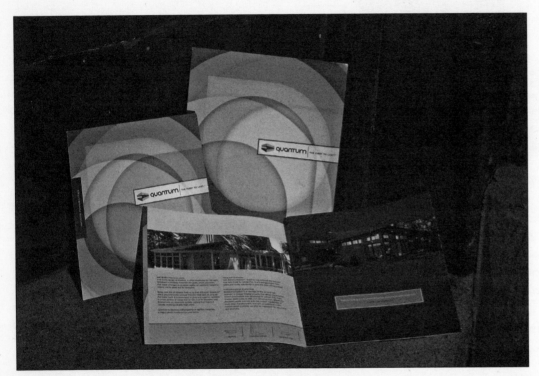

Millwork isn't an industry known for appealing design marketing. In fact, its hard-edged design grids, amateur photography, and sometimes archaic design schemes seem antithetical to actually drawing in potential customers. That's why Quantum Millwork, makers of a high-tech variant of PVC trim board, wanted a sleek design that reflected the quality product it made. BANG! Creative immediately saw the connection between color and the product and put that into play for the logo, branded artwork, and collateral literature design.

Quantum™

Why It Works

Going against the grain of the industry, Quantum's design uses vector art in bold, sophisticated palettes and uses undulating lines, creating visual depth. The design reflects the quality PVC trim line that Quantum wants to be known for, including the wide range of colors they offer. In fact, the connection between Quantum's colorful line and the colors used in the marketing design are a clever play-on-color that isn't lost on the customer. BANG! Creative designed separate brochures for each target market, with one for contractors, one for manufacturers, and one with a budget line of Quantum's products. Industrial businesses tend to shy away from appealing logos and design, but they're no less important to them. Customers—in this case, contractors and distributors—want to look at something attractive when selecting their millwork, and good-looking design elements help sell the product. The brochures were immediately a hit with Quantum's field sales team, and contractors found consumer sales easier when armed with the collateral.

Success Metrics

- Quantum was into its third printing of the gold contractor piece within just a few months of completion of the design project.

- The smaller Quantum Essentials brochure offered a stripped-down, entry-level line that more than tripled the sell-through rate at distribution.

Takeaway Tip

If your industry is "industrial" and isn't big on pleasing design, that's all the more reason for your company to have an eye-catching logo and color-infused print collateral. They become a competitive advantage. Don't stick with the status quo if you want to gain market share.

92. Sharpen Your Sights: Using Clever Advertising That Makes Viewers Stop and Think About Their Needs

Northern Eye Center, located in Little Falls, Minnesota, was looking to attract the younger demographic to its practice, as well as elevate recognition in the market it serves. But the optical industry isn't known for its snazzy ads, so the project became a challenge. The firm brought in Adventure Advertising to create a series of ads that would grab readers' attention.

Why It Works

Eye doctors don't do much clever advertising, which is why Northern Eye Center ads stand out. Rather than the traditional "buy a pair, get one free" ad, this is an ad within an ad. The series of ads are from the perspective of someone looking at the ad in a magazine. One's wearing glasses, one's holding the magazine at a distance, and one is holding the magazine up close—all scenarios that people with bad vision can relate to. It's tongue in cheek, and very visually appealing.

The ad, which ran in several regional and local publications, had tremendous success thanks to its relatability, according to

Scott Mitchell of Adventure Advertising. "First, the campaign's photography and design had stopping power. The ads looked like nothing else in the publications. Second, it caused the reader to assess the difficulties they have with their eyes—adjusting materials closer or further away simply to be able to focus. And finally, short copy called the reader to do something about their vision and stop working around the issue," says Mitchell.

The ads tie in with the center's website, which presents the three practitioners of Northern Eye Center, only blurred. Hover the cursor over each to sharpen the image and get more information.

Success Metrics

- This ad campaign series was awarded Best of Show at the regional ADDY Award competition.
- Northern Eye Center successfully got the attention of the younger demographic, and it has added a significant number of new patients thanks to the ads.

Takeaway Tip

Have fun with your advertising. Don't do the tried and true. Instead, create advertising with clever images and witty copy that demonstrates the problem you can solve and invites viewers to take action to get it solved.

93. A Program for All Seasons: Creating an Overarching Marketing Theme for the Entire Year

Synchronicity Theatre in Atlanta is known for tackling productions that are thought-provoking, engaging, and challenging. For its 10th anniversary season, it produced a brochure that exemplifies its mantra of smart, gutsy, bold theater.

Synchronicity presents a series called *Bold Voices* that includes issue-oriented plays such as *My Name Is Rachel Corrie*, a polemic and powerful criticism of the state of Israel's heavy-handed treatment of Palestinians. And on the other end of the spectrum, it presents family fare such as *A Year in the Life of Frog and Toad*. Lightdaughter created a brand that bridges both extremes with an overarching theme that applies to the whole season.

Why It Works

The visual solution includes individual posters for each production that feature photographs of the actors with iconic imagery from each show. The design includes a distinctive collage style of motifs and patterns that creates an overall visual unity for the series. The use of photos of the local actors in the poster reinforces a bond between the Synchronicity players and their audience.

Success Metrics

- Total ticket sales increased 25 percent for the 10th anniversary season.
- A family series production of *Junie B. Jones* resulted in a 675 percent increase in revenue over any past family series show.

- A calendar of events included in the season brochure allowed patrons to see the wide range of productions throughout the season and encouraged crossover attendance.

Takeaway Tip

Remember that "the whole is greater than the sum of its parts." You can create an overarching design theme and style for marketing your products and services even when there's a wide range of difference in the content of individual offerings.

94. The Express Lane for Sales: A Visual Pitch Book Captures the Sales Process and Trains an Ever-Growing Sales Team

If more of those one hundred people **immediately thought of you,** would you do more business?

Of course you would! That is what advertising is supposed to do for your business—have people think of you, instead of your competition. This is exactly the premise upon which our products were developed and exactly the result that you will get by taking advantage of our program.

Go ahead, take a bigger bite out of the metaphorical market. Or of an apple . . . you are at the supermarket after all.

DEVOUR YOUR COMPETITION

How do you take a seasoned sales pitch and make it viable for a young and growing sales team? "Sales people come with bad habits," says founder Franco Cabral, chief operating officer of Adcorp Media Group. They wanted their sales force to engage with customers using their method of selling. Adcorp developed a visual marketing solution that streamlined the value proposition and made a compelling case for expanding a niche market.

Why It Works

Adam Mietlowski, designer at Adcorp, knew he could create an effective sales kit based on the expertise of Adcorp's founders. Cabral and Peter Broccole, chief executive officer, had started the company five years prior in Broccole's living room in Westchester County, New York. You might say they could sell ice cubes to the Eskimos, but there is more than just a salesman's charm involved. Over the years, Broccole and Cabral developed a strong marketing technique for selling local advertising in supermarkets. Adcorp installs kiosks and displays in heavy-traffic areas at supermarkets and puts the ads and aisle directories on shopping carts that help customers locate common items throughout the store. They call it, "Ad

placement that is guaranteed to get you noticed."

The pitch book uses large images and devotes seven spreads to the key messaging that sets the stage for the sale. Mietlowski's design makes the sales pitch more immediate and provides a great scaffolding of step-by-step sales messaging that works well with newer salespeople and enhances the presentation of more seasoned sales reps.

Cabral says that when clients see the great design and graphics in the pitch book, they know they are going to get the same caliber of design and service with their ads. And it's not just about looking pretty; the pitch book has helped the sales staff put a better value on their offering. "We were able to

raise our rates because the value of what we offered was undervalued," says Cabral.

Success Metrics

- Sales have increased 146 percent with the pitch book.
- Adcorp has doubled its sales force and now has a sales staff of 20. The pitch book has streamlined the training process, increased sales, and helped with retention.
- Adcorp now serves more than 1,000 supermarkets in 10 states, including major players like A&P, Waldbaum's, ShopRite, and Big Y.

Takeaway Tip

Being a good salesperson is one thing; training others to sell your products and services is quite another. By establishing a play-by-play pitch book that uses effective visuals to tell the story, you may create a sales force tool that standardizes your sales pitch and increases revenue.

95. Three-Dimensional Business Cards: Expressing Your Creativity on Your Business Card

Business cards are essential marketing pieces for small businesses. But what if you're an artist? How do you express your creative skills with a business card? Egil Paulsen came up with a way, creating an easel business card. The easel business card is the same size as a standard business card, but it has perforations and foldable edges.

It converts into a miniature work of art that stands up as if on an easel. It's exactly what studios, curators, entertainment production companies, artists, and illustrators need to shine the spotlight on their design skills.

Why It Works

Paulsen has converted a disposable means of sharing contact information into a portable means of expressing creativity. Now instead of tossing the cards you get at a conference (once you record the contact information digitally), you can prop up the business card easel and enjoy it on your desk. It's a natural conversation starter. "It is important to maximize the format and deliver innovative solutions within set boundaries," says Paulsen of his design work.

Success Metrics

- Paulsen's business card serves as a way to not only share his contact info but also market his services. He's been awarded new business simply by handing the card out.
- It's been so successful, he's considering launching a design-your-own-card solution online.

Takeaway Tip

Your business card is still one of the most important communication tools for a small-business owner. Make it as memorable as a keepsake and you can showcase the unique aspects of your business. Consider adding QR Codes with links to your website or Facebook page to make your communications even more interactive.

96. What's a Symchych? Accentuating a Hard-to-Pronounce Name Can Be a Winner

Political newcomer Christine Symchych wanted to run for village trustee in Fox Point, Wisconsin, against two incumbents. What do you do when nobody really knows you and your name is hard to pronounce? Dan Saal of StudioSaal took the challenge head on with a campaign that asked, "What's a Symchych?"

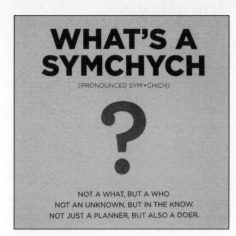

WHAT'S A SYMCHYCH

(PRONOUNCED SYM•CHICH)

?

NOT A WHAT, BUT A WHO.
NOT AN UNKNOWN, BUT IN THE KNOW.
NOT JUST A PLANNER, BUT ALSO A DOER.

Why It Works

Instead of a traditional "vote for me" campaign, Saal decided to tackle the difficult name in a bold and humorous way. Symchych (pronounced "Sym-Chich") got voter's attention with her bold campaigning materials; then, once she piqued their interest, she introduced herself and her platform with serious clarifications, "Not a *what*, but a *who*; not an unknown but in the know."

Success Metrics

- Symchych won the election by one of the largest margins in recent years for village trustee.
- The *Milwaukee Journal/Sentinel* reported, "Christine Symchych's campaign literature asked the question, 'What's a Symchych?' The answer is: The highest vote-getter in an election Tuesday for Fox Point village trustee."
- The campaign resonated with voters; one constituent showed up at a public session just so he could find out who came up with such a great promotional concept.

Takeaway Tip

Names can be hard to remember because they are unusual or difficult to pronounce, or because they are too common to leave an impression. Many small businesses use the owner's name, and if yours is problematic for any reason, address it head on in your marketing materials. Treat it with humor and visual wit to make it a positive element of your marketing—give people a reason to remember it.

97. Technology Can Be Sexy: Poking Fun at Your Industry's Stereotypes Makes It Easier for Customers to Relate

When some people think of information technology (IT) services, they think of antisocial geeks working in a basement. Iddea Group, a start-up based in Valparaiso, Indiana, wanted to break out of this stereotype and show that the virtual IT company was fun, was easy to work with, and provided quality technology services. And they wanted to make it look like they had a big marketing budget. Design firm Group 7even took the challenge on and produced a comprehensive marketing campaign that included direct-mail postcards, magazine ads, e-mails, and website design.

Why It Works

The look across all marketing channels is consistently upbeat, with bright oranges and greens, accented by Iddea Group's logo, a talk bubble. The branding does an excellent job of helping everyday business owners understand what services it provides without talking over their heads, a common issue with IT companies.

The biggest challenge for business owners looking for IT services is speaking a common language. IT experts sometimes talk in terms of servers, the cloud, and disaster recovery, while business owners want a computer system that works and can't be hacked. Not communicating in the customers' language can easily lose an IT company a sale. Iddea Group keeps it simple and relatable.

Where most IT campaigns involve heavy copy with technical lingo, Iddea Group's collateral had minimal copy as well as a teaser URL encouraging people to visit it for more information.

Success Metrics

- The campaign was extremely successful, with a 33 percent response rate.
- More than 70 percent of respondents were tracked and found to browse Iddea Group's entire website instead of clicking away.

Takeaway Tip

Embrace the stereotypes that surround your industry; then break through them to show customers who you really are. Poke fun at yourself and industry stereotypes in a tongue-in-cheek way in your marketing materials, and in the process your company will be more authentic and approachable.

98. Making Saving Look Good: Delivering Vouchers and Coupons That People Want to Save

In a global recession, how do you make more sales? In the United Kingdom, the answer's the same as in the United States: through coupons. British-based Trap Media wanted to create a voucher book targeting the educational sector, but it had to be something visually appealing that people would hang on to and use. ActuallyWeDo Design stepped in to design an appealing booklet of coupons aimed at educational institution decision makers. The result: a colorful book with images of active people popping off each page.

Why It Works

We've all received coupons in the mail, and we rarely give them a second glance. With Trap Media's booklet, each coupon begs the reader to pay attention to it, with young, happy people jumping, performing martial arts, or dancing for attention.

People, no matter where they live, like to save money. So the careful placement of "£1200 in vouchers free inside" is strategic enough to get the attention of anyone who picks the book up. And the claim isn't bogus: There are freebies and discounts that are actually attractive, which isn't always the case with coupons.

The fact that the images bleed outside the boundaries of the coupons also lends to its appeal. Many coupons are text-only and lack interesting imagery. The Trap Media booklets feature editorial-style photos that draw attention to each offer. This approach allows readers to visually scan the coupons and select the ones they are most interested in.

Success Metrics

- The project had a 2,000 percent return on its initial investment within one month of its distribution.
- The vouchers all featured a reference code so that Trap Media could monitor sales and the success of this project, helping the company determine the best-selling offers.

Takeaway Tip

Any project can benefit from good graphics and design. Just because they are coupons, discounts, or vouchers doesn't mean they need to be cheap. You can position your products and services as being about high quality not low price, even when offering discounts.

99. Good Design Flows from Product to Marketing: Creating Postcards That Are "Saveable" to Keep the Sales Pipeline Full

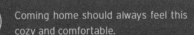
Coming home should always feel this cozy and comfortable.

Don't you just feel better when everything in your home is in its proper place?

When you're an award-winning "design to build" general contractor, you can't afford to have shoddily designed marketing. Philadelphia-based Myers Constructs, Inc., makes sure that good design is present in everything it does—from custom kitchen cabinets to direct-mail postcards. Myers uses high-quality images of its work in its series of postcards. The postcards have turned out to be essential to keeping the sales pipeline filled for 15 years for Myers.

Design to Build

An approachable renovation, such as this lovely Chestnut Hill kitchen, is the perfect update for your home during the holiday entertaining season, when friends and family gather to share traditions and reconnect.

Why It Works

The company uses attractive photos to highlight the quality of its workmanship. The postcards are so enticing that people keep the postcards, sometimes for years, and share them with friends and family. Then when it's time to hire a contractor for a project, they know what company to call.

A large part of what Myers sells is aesthetic, explains Diane Menke, vice president of production management at Myers. "This requires us to have great-looking media that tells the story of what we do. Our process is Design to Build, so obviously beautifully designed marketing materials are very important to us, as well."

Tabula Creative created the mailers with exquisite images. The photography by Jason Varney shows the final renovation in a soothing light in homes that are well cared for and decorated with a gentle touch.

Success Metrics

- During the economic downturn, Myers remained busy and even hired staff. There were no layoffs.
- Myers's website traffic in 2010 doubled compared with 2009 traffic.
- The company's overall revenue in 2010 grew almost 30 percent compared with that of 2009.
- Myers was featured in the article "The Affordable Renovation" in *Mainline Magazine*.

Takeaway Tip

When you have a long sales cycle, common for architects and contractors and other industries, create marketing materials that become coveted objects that are not easily dismissed or forgotten. Make them "saveable." People will hold onto them until they're ready to begin a project, keeping your sales pipeline filled regardless of the economy.

CREDITS

Chapter 1

1. The Color of Money: A Small Bank Makes a Large Impression with a Colorful Campaign
   Design: Leslie Evans Design Associates; photography/video: David McLain, Aurora Novus.

2. A Website Showcases a Sense of Touch: Strong Navigation and Ease of Use for an Online Showroom
   Design: Ken Carbone, principal/chief creative director, Ken Carbone; programming: Nina Masuda, designer, Carbone Smolan Agency; programmer: Atom Group.

3. Augmenting the Reality of Mobile Advertising: Sharing Brand Information Visually over Mobile Devices Through Apps
   Design: GoldRun.

4. Celebrating Creativity with a Killer Smile: Creating a Viral Marketing Effect with an Online Game
   Design: Norman Cherubino, creative director; Jim Keller, art director; and Roland Dubois, designer, Langton Cherubino Group, Ltd.

5. Putting the "Self" in Self-Portrait: Finding the Right Photo to Express a Personal Brand
   Photography: Gio Alma.

6. Luxury Property Shown in Many Different Lights: Focusing on Stunning Imagery to Sell Luxury
   Design: Doug Lloyd, creative director, Petter Ringbom, art director, designer: Dan Arbello, Flat Inc.; Identity by Pentagram.

7. How Many Ways Can You Destroy Your Printer? Going Viral with a YouTube Video Contest That Plays upon Customer Frustrations
   Photography: Nathan Dube.

8. Making a Legal Case for Insider Jokes: Using Cartoons to Market to Your Target Audience
   Cartoons for CaseCentral: Tom Fishburne, marketoonist.com.

9. Changing the Script on Scriptwriting: Organizing a Virtual Community Around an Event to Maximize Participation
   Design: Todd Blank Design; Plot Machine graphic: Jesse Reklaw.

10. When Is a Cup of Tea More Than Just Another Cup? Stunning Photography on a Website Differentiates a Product
    Design: Chris Fernandez, 5to8 design.

11. Just the Facts, Ma'am: Creating an Interactive Online Quiz Attracts a Target Audience with a Deeper Level of Engagement
    Design: Norman Cherubino, creative director, and Roland Dubois, designer, Langton Cherubino Group.

12. Getting a Leg Up on the Competition: Gaining Media Visibility for an Arcane Industry Online, Through Puns and Fun on Your Website
    Photography: Judi Townsend.

13. Building an Appealing Design: Presenting Your Process in Your Website Showcases a Competitive Advantage for an Architectural Firm
    Design: Randall Smith, creative director, and Bryan Wilson, designer, modern8.

14. A Visual Marketing Firm Uses Optical Illusions to See Things Differently: Showing Prospects What You Are Capable of in Multimedia
    Design: Norman Cherubino, creative director; Jim Keller, art director; and Roland Dubois, designer, Langton Cherubino Group.

15. Breaking Through the Gray Noise: Using a Flash-Based Presentation to Generate Leads While Also Serving as a Leave-Behind Piece
    Design and photography: Christie Grotheim, The Art Department.

16. Delivering a Unique Marketing Campaign: Combining Staged Marketing Events with Video and Social Media
    Photography: Interference Incorporated.

17. Finding Your Identity: Standing Out from the Crowd with a Website That Lets Your Personality Show Through
    Photography: Michael Persico.

18. A Renaissance for Today: Creating a Forward-Looking Logo That Reflects the Past
    Design: David Langton, creative director; Jim Keller, art director; and Janet Giampietro, designer, Langton Cherubino Group.

19. Good Service Is Earned: Making a Brand Statement and Creating Viral Content Through Infographics
    Design and illustration: Column Five Media.

20. Design to Put Your Best Foot Forward: Using Sharp, Detailed Close-Up Photography to Demonstrate Business Capabilities on the Web
    Design: Fritz Klaetke, design director/designer, and Jesse Hart, designer and developer, Visual Dialogue; photographer: Kent Dayton.

21. Spicing Up the Ornament Market: Using Bright and Unique Online Ads to Build a Brand
    Design: Darlene Tenes.

22. A Reflection of Style: Incorporating Your Business Style into Your Logo
    Design: Fritz Klaetke and Jesse Hart, designers, Visual Dialogue; photography: Kent Dayton.

23. The Right Way to Start a Charity Today: Using Facebook and Blogs to Build a Community Around a Good Cause
    Design: Jim Keller, designer and illustrator, Langton Cherubino Group.

24. Education Can Be Creative: Formatting the Standard "10 Tips" Article to Convey Professionalism and Authority
    Creative directors: Todd Turner and Chad Hutchison; copywriters: Todd Turner and Chad Hutchison; designer: Drew Bolen.

25. Dressing Down for Success: Appealing to Consumers with a Personal Video Demystifies a Confusing Subject and Builds Trust
    Design, photography, and video: Keif Oss, www.Sitepro.com; copywriting: Deborah Becker.

26. A Legal Holiday: Using Electronic Greeting Cards to Position a Law Firm as Friendly
    Design: Wilfredo Cruz, art director, Kristen Hydeck, design; Kirsten Faulder, writer; Lindsay Amat, animator; Aaron Hausman and Yelena Danilova, producers, Wechsler Ross; Mike Shapiro, illustrator, CartoonStock.

27. A Picture Speaks a Thousand Words: Creating a Visual Interpretation of What You Do in an Industry Known for Facts and Figures
    Design: Fritz Klaetke, design director/design, and Jesse Hart, designer, Visual Dialogue.

28. Walking the Talk: Making a Website That Reflects the Principles Fundamental to Your Business
Design and development: Citizen Studio; writing: Rhonda Geraci.

29. Traversing from Print to Mobile: Creating a Mobile App Version of Print for Customers with a Foot in the Mobile World
Graphic design: Brandy Wheeler; app development: Ross Rojek and Heidi Komlofske, 1776 Productions and Go Local Apps.

30. Promoting Logos with a Guess-That-Logo Contest: Tying in a Contest with E-Mail Marketing to Increase Client Engagement
Design: Norman Cherubino, creative director, and Jim Keller, art director, Langton Cherubino Group.

31. Marketing to Parents: Tailoring a Website's Look to Reinforce Your Target Niche
Design: MediaKatalyst; photography: Hope & Memory Photography, Corbis Images; illustration: Dane Storrusten.

32. Leading by Example: Using Stock Images in a Downloadable Tips Sheet to Demonstrate That Marketing Can Be Easy and Inexpensive
Design and photography: ActuallyWeDo Design.

33. Blogger Outreach in the Cloud: Using a Visually Inspired Word Cloud to Start a Conversation with a Blogger
Word cloud designs: David de Souza, using www.tagxedo.com.

34. An Illustrator Draws Up Timely Reminders for Prospects: Using Remarkable E-Mail Marketing to Keep Your Pipeline Full
Design and illustration: Robert Pizzo.

35. Bringing the Topic of Skin Care to a Head: Messaging to Teens with a Clean Peppy Web Design
Design: David Lai and Hiro Niwa, creative directors; Eunice Oh, lead designer; Makoto Chino and Hugo Zhu, technical leads; Brian Johnson, front end developer; Szu Ann Chen, executive producer; and Abbey Park Yun, project lead, Hello Design.

36. It's Not All Business All the Time: Adding a Personalized Blog Header Brings Human Interest to a Business Website
Design: Rodrigo Garcia, Palo Alto Software.

Chapter 2

54. Showcasing Talented Women: Creating a Calendar with Distinctive Photography for Yearlong Marketing
Photography: Teri Moy.

55. Get Your Clients Talking about You: Custom Designing Promotional Giveaways Makes a Big Splash
Photography: Leah Remillet Photography.

56. Breaking the Cutesy Barrier: Creating an Urban Chic Niche in an Existing Market with Displays and Packaging
Design: Christie Grotheim, The Art Department.

57. Waking Up Your Brand with a Little Pillow Talk: Creating a Follow-Up Campaign That Makes Prospects Laugh . . . and Buy
Design: Greg Daake, creative director; Sam Vetter, art director; and Steven Valish, designer, DAAKE.

58. Food Trucks, Today's Eatery Trend: Creating Cravings by Using Typography on a Truck Wrap
Design and photography: Landers Miller Design.

59. Get Me a Doctor, STAT: Using a Witty or Humorous T-Shirt to Interject Fun into How People Perceive Your Business
Design: ohTwentyone.

60. Thinking Outside the Box: Using College Lingo on an Unconventional Item to Attract Cult Status and Build Business on a College Campus
Design: Drew Hammond, art director, and Greg Ballard and Drew Hammond, copywriters, Hirons & Company.

61. An A Cappella Visual Promotion for Musicians: Attracting Your Target Market with a Banner Containing Images and No Words
Design: Bodnar Design; copywriting: Keith Oppenheim; photography: blade sign: Monika Caban.

62. Getting a Bright Start in Branding: Using Three-Dimensional Displays Integrated with a Sales Presentation
Design: Adam Bain, art director; Anthony Stephanopoulos, graphic designer; and illustrators: Charlie Mitchell, Brad Reese, and Brittany Elson.

63. Lunch Bags That Educate, Entertain, and Inspire: Maintaining a Strong Emotional Connection with Your Target Market Even as Your Brand Grows and Evolves
Designer: Kenny Kiernan.

INDEX

A

B